REVISE EDEXCEL GCSE (9–1)
History
WARFARE AND BRITISH SOCIETY, c1250–present

REVISION
GUIDE AND WORKBOOK

Series Consultant: Harry Smith

Author: Victoria Payne

Notes from the publisher

While the publishers have made every attempt to ensure that advice on the qualification and its assessment is accurate, the official specification and associated assessment guidance materials are the only authoritative source of information and should always be referred to for definitive guidance.

Pearson examiners have not contributed to any sections in this resource relevant to examination papers for which they have responsibility.

For the full range of Pearson revision titles across KS2, KS3, GCSE, Functional Skills, AS/A Level and BTEC visit:
www.pearsonschools.co.uk/revise

Contents

. . . .

A small bit of small print

Edexcel publishes Sample Assessment Material and the Specification on its website. This is the official content and this book should be used in conjunction with it. The questions in *Now try this* have been written to help you practise every topic in the book. Remember: the real exam questions may not look like this.

Composition of the army

England was at war for most of the period c1250–c1500, either in civil war or war with France, Scotland or Wales. Armies were therefore a fundamental part of medieval English society.

Composition of armies

Armies were made up of **infantry** and **mounted knights** (cavalry).

The infantry were peasants who fought on foot. They were the bottom of the social hierarchy and were treated poorly compared to other soldiers.
They may have worn skull caps and leather jackets for protection.

The mounted knights were gentry and nobility who fought on horseback and were superior in status to other types of soldier. They would have been armed with swords and lances, and protected with helmets and chainmail.

Armies had between 5000 and 10 000 soldiers. Usually, there were twice as much infantry as mounted knights.

Battlefield roles

① Mounted knights were the most powerful force on the battlefield. They weakened the enemy in the first round of attack by using:

- the **mounted charge**, charging through enemy lines to reach and kill the enemy commander
- the **rout and chase**, used to scatter enemy infantry and attack them once they were dispersed.

② The infantry's task was to hold the enemy attack and then defeat the enemy infantry.

- The **shield wall**, with overlapping shields, and spears or pikes, held enemy attacks.
- The **mêlée** was where the infantry engaged in hand-to-hand fighting with swords, pikes and daggers.

Archers were infantry who used bows or crossbows. They played a minor role working with the mounted knights to break down the enemy at the beginning of battle.

Social structure and army command

The **feudal** structure and attitudes of English society had a direct impact on how armies were commanded. Armies were commanded by those in superior social positions.

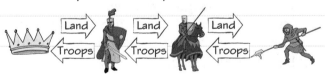

| Kings | Lords (commanders) | Noblemen and gentry (knights) | Peasants (infantry) |

Warfare was often used by kings and lords to protect their power and take power from other kings and lords. As result, warfare was usually **limited** and focused on **castles**.

A person's combat experience or skills were less important than their social status in the feudal system and, as a result, the quality of leadership varied.

Feudal system

The feudal system organised society into groups based on people's roles. Land was granted in return for service to the lord. Those serving their lord in battle provided their own equipment and provisions.

When the feudal system began to break down and it was more difficult to persuade people to fight, kings paid for soldiers to fight for them – these men were called **mercenaries**.

Now try this

Choose **one** of the following army roles: infantry, mounted knight or archer. List **three** facts to describe your chosen role in the period c1250–c1500.

New weapons and formations

The introduction of new weapons and formations had an impact on warfare, tactics and strategy between 1250 and 1500. By the end of the period, the use of mounted knights was in decline.

The longbow

In the 1290s, **longbows** were introduced into English armies. Edward I's successes made them a key part of English armies for 150 years.

- 👍 15 arrows a minute could be fired, five times more than the rate of the crossbow.
- 👍 Their increased power meant arrows could pierce through a knight's chainmail.
- 👍 They had an effective range of 200 metres, twice that of shorter bows and crossbows.

Pikes and schiltrons

The Scots under William Wallace used **schiltrons** – tight formations of infantry gathered together in a circle or square, with **pikes** facing outwards towards the enemy.

A strong defensive formation, Wallace used the schiltron to move infantry forwards and attack. The schiltron was used effectively in battles against English infantry in 1297 and English cavalry in 1314.

Gunpowder and the development of cannon

In the 13th century, the formula for **gunpowder** arrived in Europe from China. Gunpowder was used to fire **cannon** and, by 1450, cannon were becoming a standard **siege** weapon. This, in turn, affected the design of castles as old styles became increasingly vulnerable to cannon fire.

Limitations of cannon	Advantages and improvements
👎 Heavy and expensive – to transport them involved complicated logistical planning.	👍 Useful in destroying city and castle walls, shortening sieges.
👎 Inaccurate – generally they could only be used against large targets, such as walls.	👍 Improvements were made in range and aim with new technology, including trunnions (rods to raise the height of the barrel).
👎 Short range – they had to be close to their targets, making them vulnerable to attack.	👍 Specialist cannon were developed that could launch cannonballs high over defensive walls or over longer distances.
👎 Unreliable – they were likely to blow up or fail to fire.	👍 Metal was used for cannon barrels and balls, rather than stone, which made cannons more effective and accurate.
👎 Slow to reload.	
👎 Trained personnel needed.	

The mounted knight

The introduction of new weapons led to the **decline of the mounted knight** in numbers and importance. This was because:

1. the longbow was more effective in taking down knights, horses and infantry
2. the schiltron was effective at defeating cavalry, increasing the infantry's importance
3. the cavalry became more integrated, taking on specialist tasks, like patrolling and scouting, and they often dismounted to fight defensive battles.

See page 6 for an example of the impact of the longbow.

The feudal system had led to small armies in which noble knights were the superior fighters. The decline of mounted knights had important consequences for society. Instead, kings paid for mercenaries rather than relying on the nobility for their military power. This reduced the link between social class and command.

Now try this

In a short paragraph, explain why gunpowder and cannon were important developments, despite the many limitations of their use.

Recruitment and training

How combatants were recruited into medieval feudal armies changed between 1250 and 1500. There was less change in how combatants were trained for battle.

Change: recruitment of knights

In 1250, mounted knights were recruited through the **feudal levy**: knights owed 40 days' knight service and tenants owed their lords a set number of knights based on the amount of land they owned. As these dues became harder to enforce, extra forms of recruitment emerged.

1. **The Assize of Arms** was a tax on wealth, requiring all men with land to provide a number of fully equipped knights.

2. **Mercenaries and scutage** increasingly replaced feudal service and the Assize. Subjects paid **scutage** (shield money) instead of performing military service, allowing the king to hire mercenaries.

3. **The Royal Household** were permanent troops paid by the king as his personal guard. They increased rapidly in size and importance.

Change: recruitment of infantry

There was no feudal duty to serve as infantry. Instead, duty, escape, adventure or **plunder** were incentives.

1. **The Statute of Winchester (1285)** extended the Assize of Arms. All fit men between 16 and 60 were instructed to muster once a year ready and equipped for 40 days' service.

2. **Commissioners of Array** assessed recruits and their weapons across the country.

3. After 1337, the feudal levy and Assize of Arms began to fall away in favour of infantry being **paid** for their service.

For more on the feudal system, see page 1.

Baggage trains, made up of wagons and pack animals, stretched for miles behind an army.

Provisioning and equipment

In this period, demand for food and weapons for the army increased because:

- England was involved in many wars
- there were more infantrymen to feed
- more horses needed to be fed (each mounted knight took four – twice that of 1250 and archers also began to ride horses)
- more ammunition (arrows, bullets, cannon balls) was needed
- gunpowder weapons needed specific ammunition and were hard to transport.

Changes in provisioning

Combatants provided their own provisions and equipment for 40 days, but new solutions were needed to meet the increased demand.

1. **Requisitioning**: the Crown forced merchants to sell goods (purveyance) and provide ships in order to supply their baggage trains.

2. **Weapon stores**, such as the Royal Armoury, were built up.

3. **Supply depots** were set up ahead of the army and supplied by road or sea.

4. **Pillaging**, especially in enemy territory, was a common last resort.

Continuity: training

There were no permanent armies and no barracks, so no organised training for warfare.

- The Assize of Arms called for infantry recruits to be skilled with their weapons. But this was often not the case.
- Mounted knights learned military skills and competed in tournaments, but there was no training to fight as a group.
- The nobility were the military class and kings relied on leading nobles and close relatives to command their armies.

The mustering of infantry gave commanders a chance to assess their equipment and skills.

Impact of the longbow

Longbows required great strength and long training to master.
1285: Statute of Winchester set up archery targets in every town.
1363: Edward III ordered archery practice on every feast day or holiday.

Now try this

Explain why the recruitment of cavalry changed in this period.

Impact on civilians

The impact of war on civilians was mostly – but not entirely – negative. Kings needed money to pay for the wars, and they needed soldiers to fight and provisions to supply them with.

Feudal duties – taxation

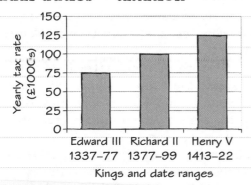

Yearly tax rate (£100Cs):
- Edward III 1337–77: 75
- Richard II 1377–99: 100
- Henry V 1413–22: 125

Kings and date ranges

The increase in tax was a burden for civilians but was probably not such a great burden compared to being recruited or having their belongings plundered by armies. The tax represented only about 1 per cent of most civilians' annual income.

Feudal duties – recruitment

- Civilians were forced to fight by the king. Desertion and refusal were common.
- Civilians increasingly chose to pay money instead to avoid going to war (scutage).
- Fighting meant time away from family and home, as well as great risk of death or injury.
- Recruits were expected to provide their own equipment and provisions for 40 days.

For more on recruitment and provisioning, see page 3.

Requisitioning

| Kings needed food and supplies (and ships) for their armies. | → | Food and fodder was requisitioned (bought by force) from civilians. This was called purveyance. | → | Civilians were meant to be paid a fair price but often weren't or were given IOUs – promises to pay at a later date. | → | Civilians suffered on two accounts:
1 They had less food and supplies for their own use.
2 They were out of pocket to the Crown. |

Benefits of warfare

War had a few benefits for civilians as well: pay was better in the army than pay for work on the land; the demand for supplies, weapons, fortifications, and so on, boosted industry and gave employment.

Fighting, plunder and its effect on enemy civilians

Sieges involved cutting towns or cities off from supplies of food and water, and – increasingly – bombarding them, forcing their surrender. This caused severe suffering for the community.

Plunder (stealing supplies from communities) gave the army food and starved the enemy.

The impact of war on civilians.

Raids on communities caused severe suffering. Sometimes the enemy was paid to go away.

Ransom (money) could be demanded from enemy communities for protection and from captives in order to secure their release.

Now try this

Give **two** ways in which warfare affected the lives of civilians in the period c1250–c1500.

The Battle of Falkirk, 1298

Case study The Battle of Falkirk was fought between the Scottish and the English in 1298. The English won due to their use of longbow archers, but the Scots also effectively used the schiltron.

Scottish infantry gather on a slope, forming schiltrons.

wood

Uncoordinated English cavalry attack separates Scottish units, driving off much of their cavalry and archers.

△ Archers

☐○ Infantry

▱ Cavalry

Red = English (14 000 troops)

Blue = Scottish (10 000 troops)

stream

Marsh area between English and Scottish.

The Battle of Falkirk on 22 July 1298 was fought to end a Scottish revolt led by William Wallace.

The impact of the longbow

Edward I's use of his longbowmen was the turning point at Falkirk and it became an essential feature of English strategy in warfare for the following 150 years.

The English were having difficulties penetrating the Scottish schiltrons, so Edward decided to use his 5000 longbows. A storm of arrows came down on the Scottish infantry. With no armour, many died.

As gaps appeared in the walls of Scottish pikes, the English cavalry were able to charge the Scottish lines. Wallace's troops fled and the English infantry joined the attack.

The impact of the schiltron formation

Wallace's schiltrons were well disciplined and the English cavalry found it hard to break through their lines of pikes. But their lack of armour left them vulnerable to archers and the Scottish archers were left isolated and exposed.

Edward I

Good decisions:

👍 Supplying his troops on campaign by sea.

👍 Outmanoeuvring Wallace to attack him from the flanks (sides of the army).

👍 Using his archers against the Scottish schiltrons.

Bad decisions:

👎 He had little control over his cavalry, but this ultimately was a fortunate thing.

William Wallace

Good decisions:

👍 Use of schiltrons.

👍 Positioning his forces on a slope, with his rear protected by woods.

Bad decisions:

👎 Failing to protect his flanks.

👎 Deciding to fight with inferior numbers.

👎 Not controlling his nobles, who deserted.

👎 Not using his remaining cavalry and archers.

Now try this

Explain why Edward I won the Battle of Falkirk. Give **three** reasons.

The Battle of Agincourt, 1415

Case study The Agincourt campaign of 1415 is part of the Hundred Years' War. The battle highlights several key elements: strategy, weapons, leadership and social attitudes.

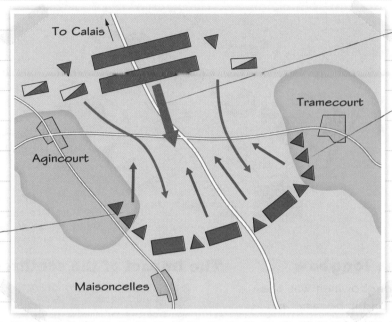

Legend:
△ Archers
▢ Infantry
◺ Cavalry
▨ Woodland
Red = English (8000 troops)
Blue = French (15 000 troops)

To Calais
Tramecourt
Agincourt
Maisoncelles

French cavalry charge in recklessly, followed more slowly by the infantry.

English forces attack the stalled French, archers joining from both flanks.

English archers, behind stakes, 'gall' the French cavalry from the two woods.

The battle was fought as Henry V's tired troops were intercepted on their way to Calais. They were weak from a long march across France and from the disease dysentery.

Choice of battleground

Henry chose the perfect defensive position.

👍 Henry's army was placed at the narrowest point of the battlefield to funnel the French into a tighter space and make it harder for them to overwhelm the English.

👍 Heavy, wet clay farmland separated the two forces, difficult for cavalry to charge across.

👍 The flanks were protected by woodland.

👍 Long sharpened stakes were set in the ground and angled towards the oncoming French, to impale charging horses.

👍 Some English archers used the shelter of the woods to fire at the French and provoke a reckless and disorganised counterattack.

Henry V

Good decisions:

👍 He was brave and fought alongside his men.

👍 He chose an excellent defensive position.

👍 He made his cavalry fight on foot, forming a solid centre to support his infantry.

👍 He sent his archers to 'gall' the French into attacking over unfavourable ground.

Bad decisions:

👍 His march across France weakened his army.

👍 He was trapped and forced to fight.

The role of cavalry and archers

① English longbowmen fired into the sides, or directly onto the heads, of the French cavalry. They could fire 100 000 arrows per minute.

② The French cavalry tried to retreat but met their own advancing infantry.

③ The French infantry were exhausted, having struggled through thick mud and over the bodies of the dead and injured.

④ The English knights fought on foot, holding the centre. The archers joined from the flanks with swords and daggers.

⑤ The English advanced, and the French were forced to retreat.

French chivalry

French knights lived by a code of **chivalry** (a code of behaviour) that dictated how they acted in battle. It focused on honourable duels between knights. The French knights were outraged at being attacked by archers, they believed this to be unchivalrous and they reacted recklessly.

Now try this

List **five** key reasons why the English won at Agincourt, despite being outnumbered.

Changes in the army

Between 1500 and 1700, warfare became more professional. Men were employed full-time as professional soldiers and were trained to fight with new weapons and tactics.

Composition

- Armies still included cavalry, infantry and artillery, assisted by labourers, engineers and baggage trains for supplies.
- Most generals still preferred about twice as many infantry to cavalry when possible.
- Changes arose as training was needed for new weapons, such as muskets and cannon, and armies became more professional.
- Artillery trains slowly increased in size and importance and field artillery improved.

Battlefield roles

Cavalry continued its specialist role, but was no longer the decisive force in battle.

- It harassed the enemy with **pistols** and skirmished with enemy cavalry.
- The mounted charge was little used until it re-emerged during the English Civil Wars.
- **Dragoons** (mounted infantry) took on the role of the mounted archer until 1700.

Infantry became dominant as result of new weapons and tactics, and was divided into two key roles:

- **musketeers** gradually replaced archers
- armoured **pikemen** increasingly fought in large, disciplined squares or columns.

The role of government

Rulers increasingly used taxes to pay for hiring soldiers. The use of mercenaries also increased. Soldiers owed loyalty to the mercenary leader who recruited them, as they had to their feudal lord previously.

Standing armies

A **standing army** is a permanent force of full-time, professional soldiers. They gave rulers a lot of power and ensured that troops were well trained.

Before the Civil War, England did not have a standing army. Parliament controlled taxes, and a standing army was very expensive. Parliament also feared a standing army would make the king too powerful. However, during the Civil War, Parliament set up a standing army to fight the king.

Strategy and tactics

Pikemen could stop a cavalry charge, but were easy targets. Pikemen and musketeers had to act together to be effective.

It took a lot of training to change formations at need. Under cavalry attack, pikemen formed a square around the musketeers. By 1600, squares were replaced by lines of musketeers that provided a volley of fire.

Oliver Cromwell

Cromwell was key in setting up the New Model Army and became the head of its cavalry. Its command structure was not traditional.

Cromwell emphasised the importance of ability and previous battlefield success over social status. The cavalry he recruited and trained formed the New Model Army's cavalry.

Timeline

Development of a standing army

1645 Parliament forms the New Model Army, a professional national army, to win the Civil War.

1660–88 Return of the king. Army continues to be retained due to the constant threat of war.

1639–40 Limitations in English militia exposed during Scottish occupation of the North of England.

1648 Second Civil War leads to Oliver Cromwell becoming Protector of England. Army retained.

1688 onwards Army 'renewed' each year to maintain principle of no standing army.

Between 1645 and 1660, the New Model Army interfered in politics and government. After 1660, the memory of this meant that it took about a century to agree to formalise a standing army (in 1775).

Now try this

Draw up a table of **three** changes and **three** examples of continuity in warfare, in the period c1500–c1700.

Developments in weaponry

The period c1500–c1700 saw big changes in weaponry. Pikes, muskets, pistols and cannon became the decisive weapons in most battles. These new weapons led to changes in battle tactics too.

Rise of the musket

Firearms were developed during the 1400s. By 1550, the musket began replacing the longbow. The musket was slow and unwieldy, so why did it replace the dominant longbow?

Developments in science and technology
New high-carbon steel armour was mostly arrow proof but armour could be pierced by muskets. Mass production of bullets meant they were available to issue to any soldier. You could store thousands in a barrel, unlike arrows, which were expensive and highly crafted.

Changes in thinking
Reports of musketeers defeating pikemen in battle led to changes in tactics.

Changes in society
Growth of towns and changes in farming methods reduced the number of archers able to train. It took years of practice to make a successful bowman; not so with the musket, which took days.

Henry VIII (1509–47) received a battle report outlining the success of German muskets against Swiss pikemen, previously unbeatable in European warfare. This led to an increase in his use of firearms.

Pistols and dragoons

In the 1540s, the **wheel-lock pistol** was developed: a smaller firearm, suitable for use by cavalry. Pistols and swords replaced the lances of medieval knights and armour was gradually abandoned as improved firepower made it redundant.

Cavalry rode close to the enemy, firing in complex manoeuvres before withdrawing to reload. Use of the charge declined. Dragoons armed with arquebuses or smaller muskets were used to skirmish and threaten an enemy's flanks.

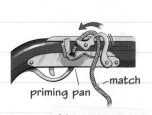

Matchlock and flintlock mechanisms

The socket bayonet fitted outside the barrel, allowing the musket still to fire

Flintlock and bayonet

By the 1690s, the **flintlock mechanism** replaced the matchlock musket. The matchlock was:

👎 dangerous near gunpowder due to its exposed match flame

👎 unreliable in rain as the match could go out

👎 visible at night due to the exposed glow.

In the 1660s, the **plug bayonet** emerged. By 1705, the pike had been replaced with the **socket bayonet**: converting musketeers into mêlée combatants so troops no longer needed to be split into two separate roles and wasted.

New technology and the cannon

The rising power of cannon was weakened:

- New engineering methods led to stronger defensive walls as protection.
- From the 1530s, England spent vast sums constructing new style defences.
- Low, thick, earth-filled walls met blows from cannon balls without shattering.
- Walls were angled, so cannon balls would bounce off without damaging them.
- Bastions provided defensive positions for the return of cannon fire.

Now try this

Explain the impact of **two** developments in weaponry in the period c1500–c1700.

The experience of war

In this period, the **New Model Army** (NMA) saw increasing professionalism in the army, with a significant impact on recruitment and training. The Civil Wars also directly affected local civilians.

Continuity in recruitment

Until 1645, the Tudor system of recruitment continued, based on the Statute of Winchester.

- All men aged 16 to 60 had to serve in their local area. They were **pressed** (forced into serving).
- Men provided their own weapons and **general musters** were held every couple of years for inspection and training.
- The king appointed Lords Lieutenant to command each county's militia.

In 1573, Trained Bands were set up from the local militia and met monthly for training by **Muster Masters**.

In the 1580s, Muster Masters were professional soldiers. Through the 1590s, they were replaced by local gentlemen, who resented taking orders from 'lowly' professionals.

Changes in training

New weapons and tactics required discipline and training: hundreds of men needed to act as one, while under fire. Early muskets were complicated to load and fire, and musketeers were trained to fight in rows or ranks. They also had to learn to work together with the pikemen.

Change: The New Model Army

In 1645, parliament raised a national volunteer army, with regular pay, that allowed successful soldiers to be promoted to command positions.

Cavalry

- 6600 cavalry were raised from existing forces; a well-trained and disciplined force that remained under control in battle.
- They received 24 pence a day but had to provide for themselves.
- They were instrumental in victory, as they held together to charge and finish an attack.
- 1000 dragoons were also raised from existing forces.

Infantry

- 14 400 infantrymen were raised, half from existing forces and half pressed.
- They received 8 pence a day, the same as a labourer.
- During 1645, desertion rates were high and 14 500 men were pressed, yet the army remained under strength.

After the Civil Wars, the volunteer army continued as a normal part of society.

The NMA introduced the uniform red coat which later became the colour used by the British army; previously each regiment wore the colour of their colonel. This caused confusion on the battlefield. The lack of a clear uniform also made it easier for soldiers to desert.

Impact of warfare on civilians

Before the Civil Wars	During the Civil Wars
• Merchant ships were requisitioned for the navy to transport soldiers and supplies. • Requisition of horses and supplies disrupted businesses and led to shortages. • Taxes increased and trade reduced, so civilians faced higher taxes and lower earnings, together with rising prices. • Damage to civilian property was generally limited to the Scottish borders, and coastal regions, where there was fighting.	• Requisitioning of ships and supplies continued. • Plunder (stealing from civilians) was very common, due to lack of pay and supplies. • Free quarter – armies forced communities to feed and house troops, leaving an IOU behind. • Both sides spent a lot and collected high taxes from the areas they controlled. • Armies could ruin crops, but sieges caused even more damage. At least 55 000 people were made homeless during the Civil Wars and many castles were partially destroyed.

Now try this

Describe **three** ways in which civilians were affected by war in the period c1500–c1700.

The Battle of Naseby, 1645

Case study The Battle of Naseby in 1645 was a turning point in the English Civil Wars. The New Model Army benefited from the decisive and inspirational leadership of Fairfax and Cromwell.

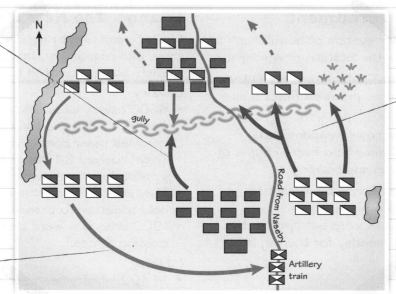

Infantry engage in the centre, Royalists have the edge.

☐ Infantry
⧄ Cavalry
⊠ Artillery

Red = Parliamentarian (17 000 troops)

Blue = Royalist (12 500 troops)

Royalist cavalry on west flank drive off the Parliamentarians and attack artillery train.

gully

Road from Naseby

Artillery train

Parliamentary cavalry, under Cromwell, beat back the Royalists but keep discipline to engage infantry flank and tip the balance.

Naseby demonstrated the strength of the NMA compared to the Royalist army.

Choice and use of battleground

The Parliamentarians positioned themselves on one side of a valley. Fairfax made good use of the terrain.

👍 The centre, Broad Moor, was a large, open expanse of common land, ideal for cavalry.

👍 His western flank was protected by a hedgerow, his eastern flank by ground that was hard to cross.

👍 He kept his men behind a ridge, out of sight of the enemy, to help morale.

👍 Their high position gave a tactical advantage as Prince Rupert was unwilling to engage musket and artillery fire head on.

Cromwell persuaded Fairfax to advance into a weaker position to tempt the Royalists into attacking up the slope.

The role of training and tactics

1 The NMA advance over the ridge to engage the Royalists as they climb the slope.

2 Prince Rupert's Royalist cavalry drive off their foes, but lose discipline and raid the baggage train for plunder.

3 The NMA infantry hold the centre, losing ground, as their frontline breaks.

4 The NMA cavalry drive off their foes, but Cromwell keeps them under control.

5 Cromwell's cavalry attack the flanks and rear of the Royalist infantry, while Fairfax counterattacks at the centre. The Royalists break.

6 Cromwell's cavalry pursues the remaining Royalist cavalry, destroying them.

Fairfax and Cromwell

👍 **Fairfax**: was an inspirational general who fought alongside his men. He led the infantry in the counterattack at the centre, gaining a vital advantage.

👍 **Cromwell**: believed NMA officers should be the best soldiers. He had recruited and trained the best cavalry in the war.

King Charles and Prince Rupert

👎 They underestimated the enemy, believing they could win though outnumbered.

👎 They wanted a speedy victory before the NMA could join the Scots, so they did not wait for reinforcements before fighting.

👎 Prince Rupert wasted his advantage on the west; he lacked control of his cavalry.

Now try this

Draw a mind map showing the reasons why the New Model Army won the Battle of Naseby. Think about leadership, strategy and resources.

Continuity and change in the army

The period c1700–c1850 saw little change in warfare. However, in the period c1850–c1900 the Industrial Revolution and the rise of the British Empire changed the scale and style of warfare.

Composition

c1700–c1850: continuity	c1850–c1900: change
• A permanent standing army of around 50 000 men, more in times of war. • The decline of cavalry continued, now only about 20 per cent of the army. • Artillery continued to form about 5 per cent.	• The growth of the British Empire meant more soldiers were needed: numbers reached 250 000 by 1899. • Governments were more involved in organising the army size and finances, both of which rose dramatically.

Specialisation and professionalisation

In this period, the armed forces were transformed into a professional organisation with a fixed term of enlistment.

c1700	c1900
• Many soldiers still pressed into service. • Marched or rode in bright uniform. • Infantry all armed with muskets and bayonets. • Support came from heavy, immobile cannon.	• Command structures more clearly defined, with specialist regiments and more effective leadership structures. • Wore camouflaged brown or grey uniforms. • Transported to battle in steamships or trains. • New weapons, such as rifles and machine guns, led to specialised roles within the infantry. • Long-distance artillery and light field artillery bombarded the enemy, using different skills.

Continuity on the battlefield

Roles	Tactics
• **Cavalry**: still important for reconnaissance and harassing the enemy, though new weapons, such as rifles and machine guns, left them vulnerable. • **Infantry**: still the decisive factor in battle. • **Infantry**: the 'Brown Bess' musket used from 1715 to around 1850.	• **Cavalry**: officers determined to keep traditional cavalry forces, seeing change as an attack on privilege – showing the importance of social attitudes. • **Infantry**: still fought in lines, columns and squares. • **Infantry**: loading times improved – four-deep lines replaced with longer two-deep lines, firing a **volley** every 20 seconds. • **Infantry**: still sent to face overwhelming firepower between 1850 and 1900; generals refused to accept the changing situation, relying on old ideas about how to fight.

Change: From around 1760, **rhythmic marching** to the drum helped infantry move and change formation quickly – generals like Wellington could use maneuvering as a tactic.

Training in this period

Various efforts were made to improve training, but had little impact due to social attitudes. Officers thought they knew best and that weapons training and tactics were easy – they resented interference. As a result, very little improvement had taken place by 1850.

Now try this

1 Name **two** ways in which the army changed in this period and explain why this occurred.

2 Name **two** ways in which the army stayed the same and explain why this was the case.

Changes in weaponry

Improvements in science, technology and industry brought about changes in weaponry and warfare in this period. These changes led to new approaches to battle strategy and tactics.

The use of rifles and bullets

Rifles	Invented in the 16th century; from 1850 technological improvements made them more effective and practical.
Minié bullets	Invented in 1847, these small bullets expanded within the barrel, making loading easier.
Conical bullets	More aerodynamic, these increased the range of rifles.
Percussion bullets	Made loading easier and rifles more reliable by ending their reliance on powder and flint.
Breech-loading	Made reloading four times quicker than with muskets.
Magazines	Allowed several bullets to be loaded at once.

Impact on tactics and formation

At the Battle of Waterloo, 1815, the British infantry formed squares to repel the enemy. By the Crimean War, 1853–56, the musket had been replaced by percussion rifles. Its increased range and accuracy meant a new defence was needed.

Development of trench warfare

In the Crimean War, systems of **trenches** gave protection against the enemy fire. Troops and supplies could move near to the front line without being exposed.

Defending forces chose the protection of the trench over mobility. The power of defensive fire was greater than that of an attacking force.

Machine guns

Small cannon-like guns, called Gatling guns, had several small revolving barrels and fired as many as 150 bullets a minute. Smaller, more practical machine guns like the Maxim were in use by the 1880s and could be moved by one man. Machine guns were introduced to the British army in 1889, but had most inpact after 1900.

Field guns and heavy artillery

Developments in technology and industry led to improvements in artillery.

Light field artillery (field guns):

- John 'Iron-Mad' Wilkinson made thinner and lighter cannon barrels.

- Experiments with bronze made cannon even lighter, with lighter carriages.

- This meant lighter, horse-drawn field guns could be used across the battlefield and moved quickly.

- By 1890, field guns were designed so they recoiled. This made firing quicker and easier.

Heavy artillery:

- Steel cannon were stronger than bronze.

- Breech-loading cannon reloaded five times faster than previous muzzle-loading cannon.

- Cannon with rifled barrels increased the range from hundreds of metres to 5 km.

- By 1900, percussion shells filled with chemicals that exploded the shell were in use.

- From the 1890s, smokeless powder stopped smoke affecting aim or revealing position.

Spiralling change: when one country improved weaponry, others would race to go one better.

Social attitudes: conservatism, fear and cost.

Factors affecting change

Political attitudes: the upheaval of the French Revolution made governments uneasy about change.

Industrialisation: improvements in science, technology and industry.

Individuals: Wellington resisted change as a threat to his social class; inventors such as Wilkinson.

Now try this

Explain how the development of **one** weapon impacted on war in this period.

Industrialisation

In the period c1850–c1900, industrialisation had a significant impact on warfare, rapidly changing transport and weaponry. Some key individuals also played a part in this rapid change.

Steam-powered transport

Changes in transport enabled armies to operate further from home.

Steam trains:

- Steam railways enabled troops to move 15 times faster than they could on foot.
- Supplies could be moved at 20 mph rather than the 10 miles a day in wagons.
- The first military railway was laid by the British at Balaclava in the Crimea.

Steamships:

- Steamships with screw propellers sailed twice as fast as sailing ships.
- Requisitioned steamships took less than three weeks to ship men and supplies to the Crimea, where they were used in warfare for the first time.

Steamships were used in warfare for the first time in the Crimean War. Specialised coastal attack craft and new defensive techniques, like iron clad exteriors, were developed.

Science

1. The development of fulminate of mercury provided the explosive that led to percussion bullets.
2. The invention of the chemical nitroglycerine led to the development of smokeless gunpowder.

Old and new technology

The period after 1850 saw new and old technology being used at the same time: horses were still used alongside new steam trains and ships; the 'Brown Bess' musket was used alongside newer rifles.

Communications

The electric telegraph had a significant impact on communication. Governments and army staff used the telegraph to contact generals on campaign. Newspaper reporters relied on telegraph information to write their reports.

In 1854, the British started a Military Telegraph detachment within the Royal Engineers. They built and operated the first field telegraph: a 24-mile network connected eight telegraph stations across the Crimean battlefront.

Mass production

By the 1850s, metal production had improved, making plenty of iron and steel available at low cost. The introduction of factory production lines led to the mass production of identical parts. These developments enabled the government to equip the whole army with standardised, reliable weaponry at a fraction of the cost.

Technology and the role of the individual

Timeline

1774 John Wilkinson patented a more accurate boring method for creating lighter cannon barrels.

1856 Henry Bessemer patented a method of mass-producing steel cheaply, reducing the cost from £60 to £7 per ton.

1857 George Armstrong pioneered the breech-loading, rifled 'Armstrong gun' used throughout the British army.

1884 Hiram Maxim developed the Maxim machine gun, which used the firing recoil to reload the firing chamber, allowing a belt of 500 bullets to be fired before reloading.

Now try this

Draw a mind map to show how industrialisation influenced warfare in the period c1850–c1900.

Reform in recruitment and training

There were a few improvements in training and recruitment in the period c1700–c1850. However, between c1850 and c1900, the government and individuals both played a role in speeding up changes.

Recruitment problems

In 1700, Britain had a standing army. The terms of service remained unchanged.

- **Officers and promotion:** The quality of officers was unreliable because commissions were linked to social status rather than merit. High ranks were only given to nobility.
- **Other ranks:** These involved short enlistments of 8–12 years or life (usually 21 years). Incentives included pay, bounties for life service, and tavern recruitment.
- **Numbers and discipline:** The army still found it difficult to recruit enough men. In wartime, criminals and debtors were let out of prison if they agreed to serve. The quality of recruits was low and officers relied on hard disciplinary methods to keep control.

Methods of recruitment

1. **Colonels' regiments:** To avoid unrest, officers were paid to set up and equip new regiments. Regiments were created as cheaply as possible in order to make a profit.

2. **1757 Militia Act:** An overhaul of the Assize of Arms, men aged 18–50 were selected from every parish to serve in the local militia for five years.

Low pay for officers, despite the high costs of training, accommodation and uniforms, meant that there was little change in the social background of officers by 1900.

Recruiting officers ignored age and physical fitness tests to get enough recruits. In the Boer War in 1899, many recruits were underfed and physically weak.

Gladstone and Cardwell

In 1868, William Gladstone's government argued for army reform. Gladstone was prepared to pass laws to enforce modernisation.

He appointed, as Secretary of State for War, Edward Cardwell, who forced through a series of reforms against strong opposition from the army.

Professionalisation

With the **1870 Army Act**, Cardwell professionalised the army, ensuring a constant supply of trained soldiers.

- Lower ranks enlisted for 12 years: six in the army and six as a reserve soldier.
- Reserves were paid a daily rate and retrained each year.
- After 12 years, soldiers could resign or sign up for another 12 years plus a pension.

Regularisation

Cardwell's **1871 Regularisation of the Forces Act** reorganised regiments into regions, with local barracks for accommodation.

- Every regiment had two 'linked' battalions – one serving at home and one abroad.
- Each regiment's third battalion was made up of local militia.

Additionally, rations were improved, and in 1881 branding and flogging were abolished.

Improved training after 1850

- By the 1860s, more officers came into the army via the Royal Military College (RMC) at Sandhurst.
- Artillery and engineering officers trained at the Woolwich Royal Military Academy from 1741.
- The Senior Department of the RMC trained existing officers.
- In 1871, the sale of commissions ended: promotion depended on merit alone.
- Military schools opened at Hythe (1853) and Shoeburyness (1859) to train weapons instructors.

Now try this

Make a table summarising the improvements in recruitment and training in this period.

Civilian experience of war

The rising cost and scale of warfare increased the impact of war on civilians. But technology also made the reality of war clear, which affected social attitudes like never before.

Recruitment

Conditions in the army were poor at home and far worse abroad. For most of this period, the army was under strength due to a lack of recruits and desertion.

Pay was less than that of a labourer, and had to pay for a soldier's food, accommodation (in peace time) and equipment.

Between 1700 and 1800, there were no army barracks for soldiers to stay in. As the size of the army grew, towns and cities increasingly met problems, with large numbers of soldiers causing disturbances and disrupting trade. The 1757 Militia Act was deeply resented and provoked riots when rumours suggested that militiamen might have to serve abroad.

Requisitioning and taxation

1 In 1700, the army relied upon requisitioning wagons and animals from civilians for transportation. It had no transport of its own. Ships were often requisitioned during wartime due to the cost of building them.

2 The cost of the army increased from about £1 million in 1700 to about £8 million in the mid-18th century. However, the burden caused by the extra cost was relatively small as the population grew and the standard of living rose. In wartime, taxes rose considerably: the wars against France, 1793–1815 cost around £25 million a year.

See page 14 for more on the Militia Act of 1757.

Impact of newspaper reporting

In 1815, *The Times* sold 5000 copies a day; by 1850, this had risen to 40 000. National papers and 500 new provincial papers were distributed across Britain by its steam train network.

William Howard Russell, of *The Times*, sent short dispatches by telegraph from the Crimea to London. It took only five hours, compared to 20 days by sea. He sent almost daily reports. Newspapers sent 300 journalists to the Boer War (1899–1902). As a result, more information reached the public than ever before; in turn, public interested boosted newspaper sales. Films showing reconstructions of the Boer War were shown in music halls – even those who couldn't read could now follow the news.

Developments in requisitioning

Requisitioning was unpopular and impractical away from Britain in distant lands.

✓ In 1855, the Land Transport Corps (later renamed the 'Military Train') was created to provide transport to the army.

✓ In 1888, the Army Service Corps took on the provision and transport of military supplies, with specially trained recruits.

Impact of war photography

Roger Fenton's photographs from the Crimean War (1853–56) brought war to life for the British public and had a big impact on public opinion. They showed first-hand the conditions soldiers encountered while serving their country.

Camp of the 5th Dragoon Guards in harsh winter conditions, by Roger Fenton

Public attitudes

Attitudes in society: successes bred jingoism and imperialism, some turned to pacifism.

Crimean War: public criticism of leadership in the press led government to resign.

Boer War: concerns over quality of recruits due to army performance led to calls for change.

The press inspired the public to make a contribution, donating time or equipment.

The Times fund for sick and wounded soldiers raised £5000 in a week (equivalent to £3 million today).

Now try this

Explain **three** ways in which the impact of warfare on civilians increased in the period c1700–c1900.

The Battle of Waterloo, 1815

🔍 Case study The Battle of Waterloo saw the famous British commander, the Duke of Wellington, inflict Napoleon Bonaparte's final defeat. Wellington's leadership proved decisive.

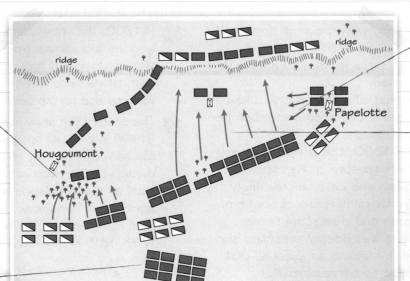

2000 Coldstream Guards hold up 13 000 in French 'diversionary' attack.

British field artillery lay down heavy fire into French flanks.

French main attack in columns into English guns.

☐ Infantry
◨ Cavalry

Red = British and allies (67 000 troops)

Blue = French (70 000 troops)

Imperial Guard in reserve.

ridge

ridge

Hougoumont

Papelotte

The Battle of Waterloo, 1815, in present-day Belgium, included many features that were typical of warfare in this period.

Choice and use of battleground

Wellington chose a good defensive position.

👍 The battlefield was good for defence as it was only about three miles across.

👍 He deployed his men behind a ridge to reduce the damage done by enemy artillery.

👍 He set up two positions on the flanks of the ridge to interrupt the French attack.

👍 He concealed field artillery in the village of Papelotte on one flank.

See page 6 to compare this with the defensive preparations of Henry V at Agincourt.

The tactics and battle

1. Napoleon attacked with infantry columns, cavalry charges and heavy artillery. The columns were 200 men wide, and could punch through lines, but lacked firepower and were big targets.

2. Wellington used 20 infantry squares each 60 metres across, with muskets and bayonets to hold back the French cavalry. The field artillery and the wounded were protected inside the squares.

3. Wellington then sent in the cavalry and infantry in lines, firing devastating volleys.

The Duke of Wellington

Wellington's tactics were successful:

👍 He prepared to defend his position. He needed to avoid being beaten until he was reinforced by the Prussian army.

👍 He used squares for defence, with cannon on the corners and infantry firing in rotation – hard to break.

👍 He switched from defence to attack just in time and personally led his troops into the fiercest fighting. Cavalry were deployed behind the advance to discourage desertion.

Napoleon Boneparte

Napoleon made some important errors:

👎 Suffering with piles and irritable, he was unable to properly assess the battlefield.

👎 He used 33 000 men to slow the Prussians; they returned late, exhausted.

👎 He delayed the start as he believed the battlefield was too muddy for cavalry.

👎 His unsuccessful attack on Hougoumont tied up a quarter of his infantry.

👎 Late in the afternoon he launched another attack when he could have withdrawn.

Now try this

Explain how Wellington's strategy and tactics helped to secure British victory at the Battle of Waterloo.

The Battle of Balaclava, 1854

Case study The Battle of Balaclava was a Russian attack on a British-held port in the Crimea. The British fought off the Russians, but needlessly launched a costly cavalry charge.

2000 Russian cavalry charge the Thin Red Line; later 3000 Russian cavalry encounter the Heavy Brigade as they advance to support the British infantry.

Light Brigade (cavalry) Russian advance forces Turkish troops off the ridge.

Heavy Brigade (cavalry)

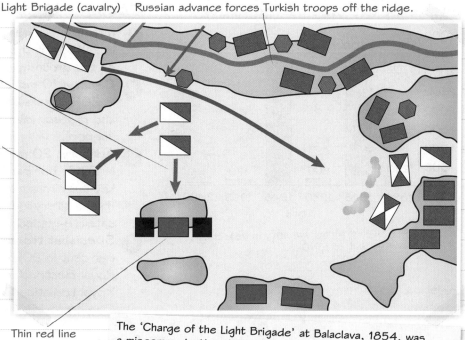

☐ Infantry
◣ Cavalry
⊠ Artillery
⬡ Redoubt (fort)

Red/Black = British and allies (3000 troops)

Blue = Russian (28 500 troops)

Thin red line

The 'Charge of the Light Brigade' at Balaclava, 1854, was a miscommunication that led to many deaths. It showed the vulnerability of the cavalry when faced with defensive firepower.

Tactics weapons and supplies

- The 93rd Highlanders under Sir Colin Campbell, using Minié rifles, held a defensive position against an attacking force of Russian cavalry.
- The soldiers, in two-deep lines in their red tunics, formed a 'thin red streak, tipped with steel', outnumbered four to one.
- Their devastating volleys drove off the cavalry. The Heavy Brigade then moved in and defeated a large force of Russian cavalry.
- The use of old methods, like a cavalry charge, against a defensive line of infantry armed with the latest rifles led to a huge loss of life.
- The power of defence became a central characteristic of warfare in this period.

Charge of the Light Brigade

- Later in the battle, the Russians began to remove the allied cannon they had captured on the ridge.
- Lord Raglan ordered Lord Lucan to recapture the cannon, but the orders were vague and poorly explained. In the confusion, Lucan thought he was being asked to attack the Russian cannons.
- Despite the uncertainty, Lucan ordered Lord Cardigan's Light Brigade to charge the Russian cannon.
- Out of 673 men in the Light Brigade, 113 were killed, 134 wounded and most of the horses had to be destroyed, for no gain.

A military railway and steamships transported British supplies during the campaign.

Lord Raglan

Raglan's actions at Balaclava showed the disadvantages of commissions that were bought rather than earned. Raglan made many mistakes:

- He knew about the build-up of Russian forces but did not reinforce his defences.
- He was heavily criticised in the British press because of shortages of clothes and supplies.
- He delayed the attack on Sebastopol, giving the enemy time to build their defences.

See pages 6 and 16 to compare Raglan's leadership with that of Henry V and Wellington.

Now try this

The Battle of Balaclava showed features of older and more modern warfare. List **two** older features and **two** newer features.

The modern army

Warfare has changed dramatically since 1900 and this is shown in the composition of the army. New units have developed to deal with the changing nature of modern warfare and technology.

Change in the size of the army

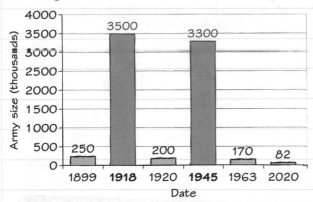

Army size (thousands) vs Date:
- 1899: 250
- 1918: 3500
- 1920: 200
- 1945: 3300
- 1963: 170
- 2020: 82

Britain has a small professional army in peacetime: a similar size to that of 1840.

Logistics refers to the transportation of troops, supplies, ammunition and post.

Growth of logistics corps

Timeline

1914–18 Scale of the First World War led to improvements: the Army Service Corps.

1993 Royal Army Service Corps joined with other army corps: Royal Logistics Corps (RLC).

- **1900** Army logistics badly organised.
- **1939–45** Second World War logistics were even more demanding.
- **2003** 15 per cent of the British army, the RLC organised logistics for the invasion of Iraq.

Changes in composition

1. **Infantry**: 65 per cent in 1914; 25 per cent in 2015; still the troops most likely to fight on the ground.

2. **Cavalry**: 10 per cent in 1914; 10 per cent in 2015 (**tanks**); tanks now lead the attack, and protect infantry and give mobile artillery support.

3. **Artillery**: 20 per cent in 1914; 10 per cent in 2015; bombarding the enemy is still key but aircraft and tanks now share this role; artillery is now more mobile, such as satellite-guided missiles.

4. **Specialist troops**: 5 per cent in 1914; 55 per cent in 2015. The Royal Engineers and Royal Electrical and Mechanical Engineers, Royal Logistics Corps and Royal Medical Corps provide support to the front.

Specialised bomb disposal units

Early 1940, 25 army bomb disposal units were formed during the Second World War.

Late 1940, another 109 bomb disposal units were created: an essential part of modern war.

In 1972, a remote-controlled robot was developed that was able to move an explosive device.

In 2015, the British army had about 2000 Explosive Ordnance Disposal (EOD) specialists.

EOD units make munitions safe after wars are over. Most bombs are still made safe by disposal experts.

Changes in structure

Two reforms shaped the structure of the modern army:

Haldane's Reforms, 1908 Response to Boer War (1899–1902)	Professional army: 150 000	Territorial Force: national reserve of part-time soldiers; renamed Territorial Army in 1920.
Army 2020 An ongoing review	Professional army: 82 000	Territorial Army renamed as Army Reserve in 2013; 30 000 part-time soldiers.

Now try this

List **five** changes in the composition of the army from 1900 to the present.

Impact of modern developments

Since about 1900, change in the nature of warfare has been ongoing and rapid. Weapons have changed as a result of new scientific discoveries, new technology, and the growth of industry.

Weaponry

1. **Machine guns:** were clumsy; needed teams of men to cool them down; very effective in defence; could fire 600 rounds a minute.
2. **Tanks:** by 1918, cavalry replaced by motor vehicles, particularly tanks, which were effectively mobile artillery.
3. **Chemical weapons:** 146 chemical attacks in First World War using chlorine, phosgene and mustard gas; most nations have now agreed not to use chemical weapons.
4. **Nuclear weapons:** In 1945, atom bomb revolutionised the power of bombing; in 1950s and 1960s, nuclear arms race between USA and USSR threatened 'Mutually Assured Destruction'.
5. **Aircraft:** British Flying Corps had 63 aircraft in 1914, 22000 by 1918; played key role as mobile artillery, providing mobility and offence.

Transport

Developments in transport means that 'defence' became less important in war.

1. 1914: Germans moved troops by **train** for surprise attack; over two million men and 600000 horses out-manoeuvre French and advance 300 km.
2. 1918: **motorised transport** introduced; British Army has over 55000 trucks and 35000 motorcycles.
3. 1940: **aircraft** parachute troops behind enemy lines; vehicles transport infantry quickly into areas seized by tanks, as with the German 'Blitzkrieg'.
4. 1944: **air support** important; allies create 'cab rank' system (aircraft always in sky), allowing infantry to call quick air strikes to weaken resistance.

Surveillance

From 1900, surveillance from aircraft was introduced. In 1957, the first artificial satellites allowed surveillance from space. Military satellites are used to:

- spot enemy forces and identify targets
- predict weather conditions
- photograph the impact of attacks
- provide communication systems.

Surveillance technology is now used to guide inter-continental ballistic missiles (ICBMs) and bombs dropped from 'stealth' aircraft, fighter jets and drones. 'Smart' bombs are 10 times more accurate than conventional bombs.

RADAR (RAdio Detection And Ranging) was vital for Britain's victory in the Battle of Britain, 1940. It was used as part of an early warning system to detect enemy aircraft.

21st-century guerrilla warfare

Powerful states can use bombing and elite infantry to capture territory, but controlling it can be more difficult.

Weaker forces may use guerrilla warfare against occupying troops. Guerillas blend in with local civilians and use hit-and-run raids instead of open battles. Traditional weapons and tactics are much harder to use against them – as the West has found in Afghanistan and Iraq.

High-tech warfare

Computerised high-tech weapons are having a significant impact. Used to attack from thousands of kilometres away, they are followed by infantry. Troops are supported by tanks, jets, attack helicopters and mobile artillery. Battles are coordinated via radio communication and satellite surveillance.

Now try this

Choose **two** ways in which science and technology have impacted warfare since 1900. In each case, explain the impact.

Modern recruitment and training

Recruitment reached an unprecedented scale during the World Wars, as 'total war' impacted civilian and soldier alike.

Changes in recruitment

> **1914-18, First World War**
> **1914:** thousands needed to replace casualties – appeal for volunteers.
> **1916:** Military Service Act introduces conscription for unmarried men aged 18–41, and later married men.
> **1918:** conscription ends.

> **1939-45, Second World War**
> **1939:** National Service Act reintroduces conscription.
> **1941:** conscription also applies to men aged up to 51, and unmarried women aged 20–30.
> **1943:** age limit for conscripted women increased to 51.

> **1960s**
> Return to permanent, volunteer standing army.

Other methods of recruitment

1. **Government propaganda** encouraged men to **enlist** (join up), but the scale of casualties put off recruits.

2. **PALs Battalions** were made up of local volunteers from the same community.

3. **National service** (introduced in 1948) meant all men aged 17–21 had to complete 18 months' military training and service, followed by four years in the Reserves.

> **Conscription** is where people **have to** serve in the armed forces, rather than volunteering.

Recruitment of women

Women were recruited into the forces for the first time during the World Wars.

Timeline

1916 Women worked as nurses in Voluntary Aid Detachments behind the front line.

1917–18 Women were recruited into the armed forces in the Auxiliary Corps, Women's Royal Naval Service and the Women's Air Force.

1941 Unmarried women aged 20–30 could be conscripted. The Women's Voluntary Service (WVS) had one million civilian members.

1944 212 000 women served in a range of uniformed military-based roles.

1992 Women were integrated into 'male' units.

The loss of life in the World Wars was extraordinary:
- 1914–18 – c10 million combatants
- 1939–45 – c15 million combatants; c45 million civilians.

A professional army

Britain has developed a regular, professional army, which currently has about 85 000 combatants. Including the RAF and the Royal Navy, the total permanent, full-time force is about 150 000 people.

- Pay and conditions match other careers.
- High-tech equipment means a high level of training and skill.
- Recruits sign up for at least four years. Basic training lasts 14 weeks. Training for specialist units takes longer.
- Over 80 per cent of officers join as graduates and train for about a year.
- The Territorial Army (or Army Reserves) provides a trained reserve force.

'Total war'

The developments in scale and weaponry led to wars of attrition, where an enemy is worn down until it runs out of manpower and resources. This gave rise to 'total warfare' where civilians were attacked as well as enemy soldiers.

Now try this

List **three** ways (each) in which recruitment and training has changed between 1900 and the present.

Modern warfare and civilians

Total war meant that all civilians were duty-bound to play their part in the war effort. This involved wide-scale government involvement in all aspects of people's lives and the economy of the country.

The impact of active fighting

1 **Recruitment:** For the first time since the medieval period, civilians were forced to take up arms in the total warfare of the 20th century. Six million Britons fought and 700 000 died in the First World War; about 450 000 died in the Second World War.

2 **Organisation of Home Front:**

- **The Home Guard** was a part-time, volunteer force formed in 1940 to defend against invasion. By 1941, 1.6 million civilians had joined.

- **The Civil Defence** volunteers defended the country from air raids from 1941. By 1945, 1.4 million wardens served and 7000 staff had been killed in the line of duty.

- **The Women's Voluntary Service** (WVS) supported the Civil Defence with its million volunteers from 1941.

> The **Home Front** refers to the civilian population and the preparations of a country at home whose forces are fighting abroad.

Living on the Home Front

1 **Rationing:** In April 1917, Britain only had a few weeks of wheat supplies left, as the Germans tried to cut off food supplies. Rationing of food items was introduced in 1918 and, again, in January 1940.

2 **The Blitz:** Between 1940 and 1941, two million British homes were destroyed and 1.5 million civilians evacuated due to German bombing. In the major cities, air raids were a constant threat.

3 **Government powers** greatly expanded during the World Wars. The Defence of the Realm Act of 1914 allowed the government to censor information and take control of key industries. The Emergency Powers Act of 1940 gave the government unlimited powers to act. Workers could be forced to move into job roles more vital to the war effort.

4 **Air-raid precautions:** During the Second World War, gas masks were issued to every civilian and air-raid shelters were set up in public spaces and in family gardens. Children were evacuated from major towns and cities. Blackouts and curfews were enforced to prevent targets from being visible to bombers.

Recruitment to the Home Front

During the Second World War, men could opt for work in the mining industry rather than join the armed forces. Those that did were called 'Bevin Boys' after the Minister of Labour, Ernest Bevin.

Unexpected benefits

Modern warfare has also brought some unexpected benefits, for example: major medical advances due to the need to treat casualties and advancements in equality for women as they took on the same jobs as men on the Home Front and in the armed forces.

Fear of a potential nuclear attack post-1945

Nuclear defence booklets were issued to the public to prepare them in case of attack.

Air-raid sirens were regularly tested and civil defence films shown in schools and cinemas.

By 1949, the two 'superpowers' (the USA and the USSR) had nuclear weapons.

Constant tension and rivalry until the 1970s led to increasing fears of nuclear war.

Central London, 1958. Organised by the Campaign for Nuclear Disarmament, thousands protest about the threat of nuclear war.

Now try this

Describe the changes for civilians on the Home Front in the Second World War compared with the First World War.

Attitudes in society

Attitudes in society had a big part in shaping progress in both World Wars and the government was keen to try to control what people heard. The rise of the media radically changed that post-1945.

Attitudes to conscientious objectors (COs)

Some civilians objected to conscription for moral or religious reasons. They were tried by military tribunals and often imprisoned or forced to serve.

First World War: It was common for COs to be shunned, even by their own family members. Sometimes they received hate mail or white feathers, as a sign of cowardice.

Second World War: COs were found alternative forms of work, sometimes not even war work. They still received hostility, and lost friends or jobs.

	COs	Forced to serve	Sent to prison
First World War	16 600	About 9500	About 7000
Second World War	60 000	About 50 000 (3000 objections upheld)	About 6000

Changes in war reporting

War reporting has changed significantly:

- **1914**: one journalist (an army officer) reports from the battlefield.
- **November 1916**: five journalists allowed at front line.
- **2003**: 700 reporters part of Coalition forces in Iraq. Many more worked independently in the war zone.

New media and communications, such as television, satellite links and the internet, have revolutionised reporting – and this in turn has impacted on public attitudes.

Reporting and public attitudes

In the First World War, numbers of volunteers fell as casualty figures were reported, leading to conscription in both World Wars.

Since 1945, public support for war has declined. In 2003, a million protestors marched against the war in Iraq. People are more likely to oppose the human and financial costs of war.

Now strategies aim to minimise casualties on both sides in order to maintain public support.

The BBC played a key role in keeping up morale in the Second World War.

Censorship and propaganda

During the First World War, the government used **censorship** (limiting the information given to the public) to hide the worst news from the public. Soldier's letters were read and censored.

Propaganda (information designed to influence public opinion) was used to build support for the war and encourage men to volunteer. It often suggested that all Germans were evil and had to be defeated.

In the Second World War, propaganda was a vital tool. It avoided exaggerating victories and concentrated on the horrors of war and the need to win. Morale-building posters encouraged support for the war effort. Censorship was also used. Newspapers could be shut down if they criticised the government. The BBC had a key role in informing the public and 'self-censored'.

Modern reporting and censorship

Now technology makes it harder for the government to control information. In 1991, the bombing of Iraq was reported before war had been officially declared to the public.

However, some information is still censored, and journalists sometimes still present a patriotic view. For example, in Iraq in 2003, reports were read before publication, and Iraqi civilian casualties were only reported later.

Now try this

Explain **two** ways in which public attitudes were different in the First World War compared to the Second World War.

The Western Front and the Somme, 1916

Case study The Battle of the Somme, 1916, was an attempt to break the stalemate on the Western Front in the First World War. It reveals the cost of 'total' wars of attrition.

First World War: The Western Front

By 1915, Allied and German trench networks spanned 600 km, from Belgium to Switzerland. The trenches led to a static war of attrition.

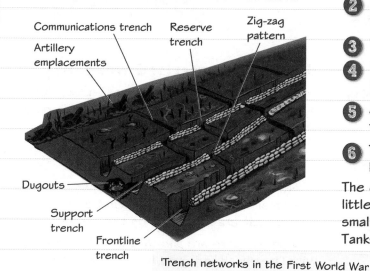

Trench networks in the First World War

The Somme Offensive

1. Royal Flying Corps shot down German observation balloons to ensure surprise.

2. Gas attacks at 40 different places along front.

3. Week-long heavy artillery bombardment.

4. 'Creeping' barrage of artillery led the infantry advance to clear their way.

5. About 120 000 infantry went 'over the top', towards the German trenches.

6. That first day, 20 000 British infantry were killed and 40 000 injured or captured.

The offensive went on for five months, with little change in strategy. Some generals tried smaller, targeted attacks, with limited success. Tanks were used, but with limited effect.

Reasons for the outcome

- Surprise was lost as the artillery barrage signalled an attack was about to start.
- The German trench system was strong and deep: 12 lines of parallel trenches and dugouts, including useful tunnels.
- Power of defence: rifles, machine guns and artillery cut down soldiers as they advanced.

- The British infantry were new volunteers and lacked experience and training.
- The British artillery barrage failed: the defences in No Man's Land remained intact.
- Tanks were poorly managed, spread over a wide area so their impact was limited.

The nature of trench warfare

- Boring daily routines, such as sentry duty and cleaning weapons.
- Frontline soldiers lived in dugouts.
- Constant wet feet led to trench foot.
- Winters were harsh and continuous bombardment meant little sleep.
- Dirty water and rats spread disease.
- Lice were common and caused trench fever.
- 'Shell shock' symptoms included crying, shaking, muteness and paralysis.

The role of General Haig

- 👍 Under government pressure to recapture lost land so needed to attack.
- 👍 Wanted to pin down the German troops at the Somme.
- 👍 Calculated heavy casualties would hit Germany harder than Allies.
- 👎 Didn't change strategy after earlier infantry attacks were so unsuccessful.
- 👎 Used new weapons badly.
- 👎 Didn't listen to advice from other generals to change his tactics.

Now try this

List **four** reasons why the trench system at the Battle of the Somme led to the lack of British success.

The Iraq War, 2003

Case study In 2003, a US- and UK-led coalition attacked the less-developed state of Iraq, using modern, high-tech forces. A guerrilla war developed and, by 2011, Coalition forces were eventually withdrawn.

High-tech warfare

The Coalition used high-tech weaponry and surveillance techniques: their strategy was 'C4ISR' – command, control, communications, computers, intelligence, surveillance and reconnaissance. For example, remote-controlled drones, like this one, kept the pilots themselves at a distance from the action.

Strategy

The Coalition relied on 'shock and awe' – using overwhelming, advanced firepower.

1 **Preparing the battlefield:** F-117 fighters bombed Iraqi leaders while missiles were launched at bases and special forces went in.

2 **Air raids:** two months of daily, targeted bombing, mostly with 'smart' weaponry.

3 **Ground attack:** 200 000 ground troops captured key cities with support from aircraft, helicopters, tanks and mobile heavy artillery.

Reporters embedded with special forces teams also deployed behind the lines and television crews reported live on the bombardment.

Use of computerised weaponry

F-117 stealth fighter-bombers are undetectable by radar. Britain's main aircraft was the Tornado. They were used to deliver 'smart' bombs:

- Paveway bombs are 'smart' bombs, guided using lasers and satellite guidance (GPS).
- Storm Shadows are cruise missiles launched from aircraft, guided by ground operatives using cameras installed on the missile.

Challenger tanks are the UK's main battle tank. With laser-assisted guns, they fire eight shells a minute. On 27 March 2003, Challengers destroyed 14 enemy tanks without loss. Iraqi tanks lacked the power and armour to compete.

Coalition aircraft also dropped propaganda leaflets urging the Iraqi forces to surrender.

Aerial surveillance techniques

1 Directed by pilots from the ground via cameras, drones were used for reconnaissance and bombing missions.

2 Satnet 1, the UK satellite network over Iraq, was used to intercept Iraqi communications, and to provide real-time pictures of the ground and early warnings of Iraqi attacks. Satellites were also used to guide 'smart' bombs, using GPS.

Instead of watching from high ground, modern commanders watch battles unfold from space. This is a significant change in modern warfare.

Reasons for the outcome

The Coalition defeated Iraq's army in 20 days, but had to withdraw eight years later. They had advanced weapons technology which easily dealt with Iraq's outdated weapons such as the 1958-model T-55 tank. Iraq's air force stayed grounded rather than confront Coalition aircraft.

However, the high-tech weapons and tactics were not effective for controlling the country after Iraq's army was defeated. Guerrilla fighters attacked Coalition forces with hit-and-run raids, suicide attacks and improvised explosive devices (IEDs). These tactics caused thousands of casualties and sapped morale. Total victory was never achieved and Coalition forces were eventually withdrawn.

Now try this

In a table, summarise the changes in warfare as a result of the Iraq War. Think about the different types of weapons and surveillance techniques and how these were used by the Coalition forces.

London: a target city

When war broke out in 1939, London was expected to be a target for German attack. After a few test raids, the 'Blitz' finally began on 7 September 1940, as Hitler prepared for a planned invasion of Britain.

The context of London in the Second World War

London was an important target for the Germans: it was the seat of government, the capital city, and the home of the royal family. It was also a major port and transport hub, a centre for industry and it was densely populated. London's fall could have a dramatic effect on Britain's Empire.

Accessibility for German bombers

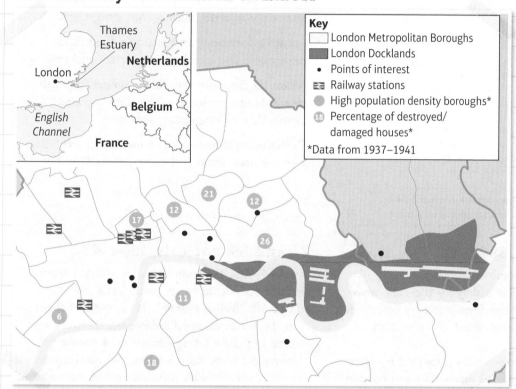

Key
- ☐ London Metropolitan Boroughs
- ▨ London Docklands
- • Points of interest
- ⇄ Railway stations
- ◯ High population density boroughs*
- ⑱ Percentage of destroyed/ damaged houses*

*Data from 1937–1941

The Thames and its estuary made an easy route-finder for pilots. In night raids, the moonlight shone on the Thames, which was clearly visible from the air. The area was also close to the Channel and therefore near to occupied Europe.

Created in September 1939, based in London, the Ministry of Information was a central government department responsible for propaganda and publicity.

Preparations for war, 1939

Planning was shared between the London County Council (LCC) and 28 borough councils.

- Gas masks had been issued to all Londoners following the 1938 Munich Crisis.
- The Air-Raid Precautions Act required local governments to set up air-raid precautions (ARP).
- The LCC organised Fire, Ambulance and Heavy Rescue Services and care of homeless.
- The boroughs set up local ARP wardens.
- In January 1939, there was a drive to recruit volunteers – together called Civil Defence.
- London children were to be evacuated into the country by school from 1 September.
- The National Service brochure offered fees for rural families willing to take in evacuees.
- In a policy of dispersal, families were offered Anderson shelters or space in communal shelters if they did not have a garden.

Propaganda and censorship

London civil servants created propaganda and ensured censorship effectively controlled public information.

Propaganda was used to maintain morale and encourage people to support the war effort. Part of this aimed to influence attitudes about the Blitz.

The government helped to create the 'Blitz spirit', where a united British population, from worker to royalty, weathered the storm together and stood defiant. Photographs showed the royal family visiting bomb sites.

Now try this

List **five** reasons why London was such an important target for German bombing.

The nature of the Blitz

The First Blitz targeted industry and transport: bombing was heaviest in the East End. After 19 September, all London became the target as the Germans aimed to destroy civilian morale.

Stages of the Blitz

25 August–19 September 1940
Targeted bombing of military bases, industry, energy supplies and communications.

⬇

20 September 1940–10 May 1941
Shift to attacking morale: civilians and homes, national treasures, industry, communications.

⬇

The 'Lull', May 1941–January 1944
Irregular, retaliatory raids, not every night.

⬇

The 'Baby Blitz', January–April 1944
Few raids got through in these last attacks, but monthly casualties jumped from 58 to 948.

⬇

V1 and V2 raids, June 1944–March 1945
German attacks switched to pilotless aircraft.

Black Saturday, 7 September 1940

- The First Blitz truly began around 5 p.m. on 7 September and lasted until 10 May 1941.
- The first attack lasted about 12 hours.
- Over 400 people were killed and 1600 seriously injured during that one night.
- Attacks focused on London's East End especially the docks, industries and railways.
- After 19 September, raids aimed for high death tolls, serious urban damage and disruption of essential services.
- Conventional heavy bombing killed 28 556 people and wounded over 25 500 in total.

On 29 December 1940, incendiaries caused over 1500 fires in central London.

Types of bombs, 1940–41

Three main types of bomb were used:

- **Incendiaries**: dropped mainly by the first wave of bombers; started the fires used by bombers as targets; fires caused about 90 per cent of bombing damage.
- **High explosives**: were mainly dropped by later waves; some had delayed fuses to harm rescue workers.
- **Mines**: the most powerful; dropped by parachute so attacks were silent and hard to detect.

The government censored information about these rockets at first, as they did not want to cause panic.

The impact of the V1 and V2s

- Civilian morale very low and factory workers were often absent from work.
- More evacuations began and the Underground filled with civilians seeking shelter.
- The government's popularity fell as people felt unprotected.
- Over 30 000 houses were destroyed and almost 29 000 people were killed or injured.

V1 and V2 rockets, 1944–45

In 1944–45, German attacks shifted from aircraft to pilotless 'rocket' attacks.

- **The V1 'flying bomb'**: hit London targets in daytime; caused extensive damage and deaths; didn't trigger air-raid warnings because they flew so low, so getting to air-raid shelters was difficult; most casualties caused by flying glass from explosions.
- **The V2 rocket**: the first ballistic missile (a rocket carrying a warhead); so fast that it exploded before people heard it coming; attacks continued until the launch sites were captured by the Allies in Europe.

The V2 attack on Deptford, 1944

On 25 November 1944, the first V2 attack to be widely reported hit New Cross, Deptford. Woolworths, a large store, was struck on a Saturday lunchtime when many were shopping. About 160 people were killed and 200 injured.

Think about the targets of the bombing, as well as the weapons used.

Now try this

Write a paragraph to explain how the nature of the bombing raids on London changed during the war.

Impact on civilian life

Civilian daily life was affected in every way possible. Many efforts were made to carry on life as normally as people could in the circumstances, including keeping up morale by enjoying leisure time.

Air-raid precautions

Government policy on shelters changed over time. Underground stations were opened due to public demand for deep shelters. Conditions gradually improved and beds were set up. Although the public felt safer in Underground stations, some were hit by bombs.

> News of Tube station disasters was censored to stop the Germans finding out the effects of their bombing and to protect morale.

Communal shelters were often overcrowded. In Spitalfields, local optician Mickey Davis formed a committee to run the local shelter – **'Micky's shelter'** – providing cleaning, beds, GP services and a canteen. In March 1941, the Morrison shelter came in.

> These disasters show how the government censored information they believed would harm morale.

The South Hallsville School disaster, 1940

About 1000 homeless Londoners were staying at South Hallsville School on 10 September 1940 when it was hit in a bombing raid. They had been due to evacuate the day before. The reporting of the incident was banned because of the impact on morale. Casualty reports varied widely.

The Bethnal Green disaster, 1943

On 3 March 1943, after a heavy Allied raid over Germany, 1500 people used the Bethnal Green Tube shelter as they expected a revenge attack. New anti-aircraft rockets were fired from nearby, causing panic. A woman with a baby fell, and 173 people died as people pushed to get to safety. Government investigations were kept secret until after the war.

Continuing leisure activities

Cinema	Wartime audiences increased by more than half; a useful tool for promoting propaganda and unity.
Dance halls	Large dance halls stayed open throughout the war.
Football	Crowds were limited to 8000 in London. Many professionals played in exhibition matches.
Theatre	Late afternoon performances and government-subsidised lunch concerts proved very popular.

Government and morale

The first weeks of the Blitz intensified class tensions as the working-class East End suffered most. The Underground was focused in the richer West End, and thousands went there in search of shelter. Tensions eased as the German bombers shifted their focus.

The government censored the information released to the public. Propaganda campaigns (films and posters) were used to boost morale, encourage 'safe' behaviour, increase support for the war, and warn against spies.

A system of food and clothes rationing was introduced.

The population of inner London fell as those who could, moved to safer areas.

Limited transport and night-time blackouts made getting to work and travel difficult.

Unexploded bombs kept people away from their homes until they were made safe.

Disruption to daily life and work

Bombing disrupted gas, electricity and water supplies.

Civil Defence volunteers dealt with death and horrific injuries on a massive scale.

More than 54 000 people were killed and injured from September 1940 to May 1941.

In the first six weeks of the Blitz, around 250 000 Londoners were made homeless.

Now try this

Explain **three** ways that civilian morale was kept high during the war.

London's response

The government wanted to keep the level of morale in London high and introduced measures that helped Londoners in their everyday lives as they coped with the experience of the Blitz.

How did London cope with the war?

Continued presence of the royal family

- Stayed in London during the Blitz: stayed visible, visiting bombed communities, boosting morale.
- King George VI and Queen Elizabeth were pictured among the rubble at Buckingham Palace following a hit there.
- Presented Britain as united, with even the most privileged suffering 'equally'.

The Cabinet War Rooms

- Government stayed in London so as not to be seen as 'abandoning' Londoners.
- The Cabinet War Rooms sheltered Churchill and his wartime government from the Blitz.
- From these rooms, the government led the war. The Map Room was the centre of activity.

London's response to war

Safeguarding art and buildings

- Protecting landmarks and national collections was important for morale.
- Some museums and galleries set up special underground storage: the National Gallery sent paintings to a Welsh quarry; the British Museum stored treasures in an unused Tube station.
- Sandbags were used and stained glass windows removed to protect key buildings, but some were destroyed.
- The survival of St Paul's Cathedral became a symbol of London resistance, with special fire-watchers and stores of water set up in the building.

The use of public spaces: 'Dig for Victory'

- 'Dig for Victory': a government campaign set up by the British Ministry of Agriculture. Civilians across the country were encouraged to grow their own food because of shortages and rationing.
- Public spaces, like Victoria Park in Hackney, were turned into allotments. The green areas in front of the Tower of London were turned into vegetable patches.
- Posters and leaflets were produced as part of a countrywide propaganda campaign intended to ensure that people had enough to eat, and that civilian morale was kept high.

See pages 20–21 for more on how London's volunteers responded in the Home Guard (Land Defence Volunteers) and Civil Defence forces.

You could refer to pages 21 and 25, as well as this one, to help you answer this question.

Now try this

In a table, summarise the measures used by the government and how these helped civilians to cope with the Blitz. For example, think about gas masks, shelters and rationing.

Exam overview

This page introduces you to the main features and requirements of the Paper 1 Option 12 exam paper.

About Paper 1

- Paper 1 is for both your thematic study (Section B) and your study of a historic environment (Section A).

- Section A will be on London and the Second World War, 1939–45.

- Section B will be on Warfare and British society, c1250–present.

- You will receive two documents: a question paper, which you write into, and a sources booklet, which you will need for some questions in Section A.

> The Paper 1 exam lasts for 1 hour 15 minutes (75 minutes) in total. You should spend about 25 minutes on the historic environment and 50 minutes on the thematic study.

> You can see examples of all questions on pages 30–37, and in the practice questions on pages 38–54.

The questions

The questions for Paper 1 will always follow this pattern.

Section A: Question 1

Describe **two** features of …   **(4 marks)**

> Question 1 targets AO1. AO1 is about showing your **knowledge** and **understanding** of key features and characteristics of the topic.

Section A: Question 2(a)

How useful are Sources A and B for an enquiry into …?

Explain your answer, using Sources A and B and your knowledge of the historical context. **(8 marks)**

> Question 2(a) targets AO3, which is about analysing, evaluating and using sources to make substantiated judgements. This is where you show your ability to **analyse** and **evaluate** the usefulness of **sources**.

Section A: Question 2(b)

How could you follow up Source [A/B] to find out more about …?   **(4 marks)**

Complete the table, giving the question you would ask and the type of source you could use.

> Question 2(b) also targets AO3. This is where you show your ability to use **sources** to frame historical questions.

Section B: Question 3

Explain **one** way in which … was similar to/ different from …   **(4 marks)**

> Question 3 targets both AO1 and AO2. AO2 is about explaining and analysing key events using historical concepts, such as causation, consequence, change, continuity, similarity and difference. This question focuses on **similarity** and **difference** across two periods of time.

Section B: Question 4

Explain why …   **(12 marks)**

Two prompts and your own information.

> Question 4 also targets both AO1 and AO2. It focuses on **causation**: explaining why something happened.

Section B: Question 5 or 6

'Statement' and How far do you agree?

Explain your answer.

(16 marks plus 4 marks for SPaG and use of specialist terminology)

Two prompts and your own information.

> You have to answer either Question 5 or Question 6. These target both AO1 and AO2 and you need to make a **judgement** in each question. Up to 4 marks are available for spelling, punctuation, grammar (SPaG) and use of specialist terminology.

Question 1: Describing features

Question 1 on your exam paper will ask you to 'Describe **two** features of...'. There are four marks available for this question: two for each feature you describe.

Worked example

Describe **two** features of the government's attempts to maintain morale during the Second World War.   **(4 marks)**

What does 'describe' mean?

Describe means to give an account of the main characteristics of something. You develop your description with relevant details, but you do not need to include reasons or justifications.

Sample answer

Feature 1

The government maintained morale by using propaganda to put across a positive message.

Feature 2

People were allowed to go out for entertainment even though the country was fighting a war.

Links You can revise morale during the Second World War on pages 27 and 28.

Make sure you read the question – it's asking for features of the government's attempts to keep up morale, not reasons why this was necessary.

This is a feature but it lacks detail about how the government used these opportunities to ensure morale was maintained.

Improved answer

Feature 1

The government used a range of propaganda to promote a positive message about the war. Posters, film and radio broadcasts were used to keep the message clear and positive. They presented an image of Britain as determined and united despite the difficulties. They promoted a patriotic Britain that could endure the hardship and defeat Hitler.

This improves Feature 1 from above by adding in more detail about the messages that were put forward in government propaganda and the methods used.

Feature 2

The government allowed entertainment venues to carry on. Professional football matches were sometimes played and attracted thousands of spectators. In the evenings, dance halls were permitted to stay open as the government acknowledged that people could have some fun despite the suffering and hardships.

You need to describe two separate features as the student has done here. Feature 2 describes a separate feature of the government's attempts to keep up public morale.

Source skills 1

In your exam, Questions 2(a) and 2(b) are based on **sources**. Question 2(a) will ask you about the **usefulness** of the sources and Question 2(b) will ask you how you would **follow up information** in one source.

Usefulness

1 Content

- What information in the source is relevant to the enquiry?

- How useful is this information?

 Underline and annotate information in the source to help you with this.

 Remember that this isn't necessarily about the amount of information given. A small piece of information can be very useful!

2 Provenance

- Nature: the type of source it is.

- Origins: who produced it and when.

- Purpose: the reason the source was created.

- How do these things impact on the usefulness of the source?

 Remember that an unreliable source can still be useful.

3 Context

- Use your own knowledge of the enquiry topic to evaluate the source.

- Is the information in the source accurate compared with what you know?

 Remember to think about what information is missing from the source as well as what's included.

Following up sources

For Question 2(b) you have to complete a table like the one below.

Detail in Source X that I would follow up:

....

 This has to be related to the enquiry given in the question.

Question I would ask:

....

This must be related to the enquiry and the detail you've written above.

What type of source I could use:

....

There are likely to be many different types of source, but make sure you choose one that will really help investigate the question you've written above.

How this might help answer my question:

....

 You should write one or two sentences explaining how the type of source chosen above could help you answer your question.

Examples of sources: national

- New laws that were made.
- Government or military official records.
- National newspaper articles and reports.
- Government propaganda.

Examples of sources: local

- Village memorials for the dead.
- Local newspaper articles and reports.
- Village and church newsletters.
- Personal accounts/memoirs or diary entries.

Source skills 2

In your exam you will be given a source booklet containing two sources. Both Questions 2(a) and 2(b) require you to **analyse** the sources so it is important that you spend time reading and looking at these sources carefully before you start your answers. You could also annotate the sources to help you.

Source A: A public information poster about evacuation, published in 1939, during the Second World War.

Try to think about the historical context of the sources as this will help you understand how far it is useful for your line of enquiry.

The children are happy and smiling at the camera, suggesting a staged photograph. What was the artist or photographer trying to convey?

It's vital to read the information given about each source as this is where you'll find information on the **provenance** (nature, origin and purpose) of that source.

The purpose of a photograph can sometimes be seen by assessing what is **not** being shown. What does your own knowledge suggest might have been omitted?

If there is text alongside a visual source, you need to consider how it links to the picture. For example, here the bold use of white lettering is a clear message to parents about the benefits of evacuation. Consider the content of any message. What does the need for this type of message suggest about the intended audience?

To what extent can you trust this person to give information relevant to your enquiry? This will affect how useful any information given is.

Think about the author of the source. How does their job, background or situation impact on the way they present information?

Source B: An interview with actor Sir Michael Caine, who was evacuated from London during the Second World War, remembering life as an evacuee. The interview was published in 1988 in the collection *No Time to Wave Goodbye*, by Ben Wicks.

A personal account may or may not be representative of the general experience that people had.

How does this account compare to what you know about how evacuees were treated? The author may have emphasised some aspects of their experience over others.

The woman said, 'Here's your meal' and gave us a tin of pilchards between the two of us and some bread and water. Now we'd been in a rich woman's house before, so we said: 'Where's the butter?' And we got a sudden wallop round the head. What we later found out was that the woman hated kids and was doing it for extra money. So the meals were the cheapest you could dish up.

When you're reading the source, highlight any particularly useful information it gives that is relevant to the enquiry.

Question 2(a): Usefulness of sources

Question 2(a) on your exam paper will ask you how useful two sources are for a particular enquiry. There are eight marks available for this question.

Worked example

Study Sources A and B on page 32.

How useful are Sources A and B for an enquiry into the experiences of evacuees in the Second World War?

Explain your answer using Sources A and B and your own knowledge of the historical context.

(8 marks)

What does 'how useful' mean?

How useful means how valuable are the sources for a specific enquiry. You need to come to a judgement on how useful each of the sources is for the enquiry given in the question.

Links You can revise evacuation during the Second World War on pages 21, 25 and 27.

Sample extract

Source A is a government-produced poster that was issued as part of a public information campaign about evacuation. It has some use for understanding the experiences of evacuees in the Second World War. However, it mostly shows what the government wanted to present about evacuation as it's not from the children themselves.

Remember to include reasons why the source was created and the intended audience it was aimed at, which this student does.

It shows two children who have been evacuated. They look healthy and happy in the photograph. We don't know if this was staged or even if they were genuinely evacuated children.

Always make a **judgement** on how useful a source is and then explain why you have reached this decision. This answer has done this by saying the source is not so useful because the photograph may not be genuine.

The caption tells us it was issued by the government. In 1939, the authorities were keen to promote evacuation to help protect children from the bombing raids that were targeted at British cities. Some children were taken home by their parents as they were unhappy or the parents believed the threat was limited. The government believed that the bombing of civilians was bound to get heavier and did not want people to be complacent about their safety.

With visual sources, always give a brief description of what you can see that is relevant to the enquiry as the student has done here.

Source B is written by someone who experienced evacuation first hand ...

Use your **own knowledge** of the topic to analyse the source – this student tells us that they know that some children were unhappy and that some parents did not believe the threat was serious.

You **must** use both sources in your answer so it's good to see that this student is continuing their answer by looking at Source B.

Remember only to include information that is directly relevant to the source, which this student does.

33

Question 2(b): Following up sources

Question 2(b) on your exam paper will ask you to pick a detail from one source and explain how you would follow up that detail in another source. There are four marks available for this question.

Worked example

Study Source B on page 32.

How could you follow up Source B to find out more about the experience of evacuees in the Second World War?

In your answer, you must give the question you would ask and the type of source you could use.

Complete the table below.   **(4 marks)**

Detail in Source B that I would follow up:
'… the woman hated kids and was doing it for the extra money.'
Question I would ask:
Did all host families take in evacuees just because they were paid to do so?
What type of source I could use:
A letter from a different evacuated child.
How this might help answer my question:
This would help me see if other evacuees were unhappy too, and felt like they were taken in so that hosts could use the rations for themselves.

What does 'follow up' mean?

Follow up means investigate something further. In other words, how you could find out more information on something in one source using another source.

Links You can revise evacuation during the Second World War on pages 21, 25 and 27.

The table is provided to help you structure your answer so make sure you use the prompts as the student has done here.

Make sure the question is linked to the detail you have used in the first part of your answer.

Remember, you only need to give one type of source here. There is only one mark for each of the points so don't waste time going into more detail than is necessary.

This answer must relate to the type of source and the enquiry question you have chosen.

Question 3: Making comparisons

Question 3 on your exam paper will ask you to explain **one** way in which something was similar or different over time. There are four marks available for this question.

 You can revise the role of the cavalry on pages 1 and 11.

What does 'explain one way' mean?

Explain one way means providing details of one way in which something was similar or different over time. You do not need to explain the reasons for the similarity or difference.

Worked example

Explain **one** way in which the role of the cavalry in 1250 was different from the role of the cavalry in 1900. **(4 marks)**

Sample answer

The army in 1250 included a mixture of cavalry and infantry. Most generals wanted twice as many infantry as cavalry. The cavalry was heavily armed with a variety of weapons, including swords and lances, and was used for mounted charges against the enemy. The infantry were on foot and were armed with spears or pikes.

By 1900, the cavalry was still used in battles. Armies also used artillery and machine guns like the Maxim. These led to lots of casualties on the battlefield.

 Don't give a general description of the army as the student has done here. You have to give details of how the role of the cavalry was different.

Make sure you answer the question asked. The question is about how the role of the cavalry was different – this answer mentions the role of the infantry and their weapons, and artillery, which is not what is required.

The question asks for 'one' way so only one is needed. There is no need to give more than one.

Improved answer

In 1250, the cavalry were the elite part of the army. Their main role was as a quickly deployed force that intimidated and weakened the enemy by charging into them at high speed.

By 1900, the development of the machine gun meant they were no longer effective as an attacking force across an open battlefield. Instead, cavalry took on specialist tasks such as patrolling, scouting and raiding.

 Make sure you just give **one** way as the student has done here and focus on difference, not similarity.

 This question is only worth four marks, so long answers are not required. Spending too long on this question will mean you run out of time for the ones worth more marks.

 You need to give some detail about how the role of the cavalry specifically was different – focusing on just one way.

Question 4: Explaining why

Question 4 on your exam paper is about causation: **explaining why** something happened. There are 12 marks available for this question and two prompts to help you answer; you must also use information of your own.

Worked example

Explain why there were changes in weaponry in the period c1700–c1900.

You may use the following in your answer:

- Industrialisation
- New inventions

You **must** also use information of your own.

(12 marks)

Sample extract

Weapons technology changed significantly in the period c1700–c1900. In 1700 cavalry relied on swords and infantry relied on pikes and muskets but, by 1900, the shift to heavy artillery and the use of machine guns meant weapons had changed dramatically.

The process of industrialisation was important in explaining the change. New techniques and discoveries meant weapons technology developed. For example, scientific progress also improved weapons. The development of new chemicals like fulminate of mercury led to new knowledge of explosives.

Improved extract

Changes in weaponry in the period c1700–c1900 were affected by new methods of production. By the 1850s, metal production was much improved. Iron and steel were more cheaply and readily available, making it possible to make higher-quality, cheaper weapons. Factory production lines used machines to mass-produce identical parts at lower cost. This made weapons more reliable and cheaper to make, like the Lee-Enfield rifles, which were adopted throughout the British army.

Maxim worked on engineering an effective machine gun that was portable and could be deployed easily in battle. In 1885, he showed the British army the first automatic and easily transportable machine gun. Maxim's technical breakthrough was using the energy created by each bullet's recoil to force out the used cartridge and install the next bullet. His invention could fire 500 rounds per minute so was equivalent to 100 rifles and was adopted by the British army in 1889.

What does 'explain why' mean?

Explain why means saying how or why something happened, backed up with examples or justifications to support the reasons you give. Good ways to get into an explanation are to use sentence starters like 'One reason for this was …' or 'This was because …'

 **Links** You can revise weaponry in the period c1700–c1900 on pages 12 and 13.

It's a good idea to start your answer, as here, with a summary of what changed. Ideally, though, you would also offer a brief explanation of why this change happened, which you would develop through the rest of your answer.

You can use the prompts given in the question to help you but you must use them to explain why changes happened. This paragraph follows one of the prompts and demonstrates good factual knowledge (AO1) of scientific discoveries, but could make the link to explain new weapons more clearly (AO2).

You must link your own knowledge with explanation and you must also **use some of your own knowledge** and not just rely on the bullets provided.

The best answers will link knowledge with an explanation of change. Crucially here, this answer begins to explain the link between mass production and weapons becoming cheaper to make.

The student could develop the answer by explaining how other factors like the role of science led to changes in weaponry.

Question 5/6: Making a judgement

Question 5/6 on your exam paper involves **analysing the statement** in the question and deciding how far you agree with it. There are 16 marks available (20 marks in total when SPaG is included) for this question and two prompts to help you; you must also use information of your own.

Worked example

'The use of gunpowder was the most important development in warfare in the period c1250–c1700.'

How far do you agree? Explain your answer.

You may use the following in your answer:

- Longbows
- Matchlock musket

You **must** also use information of your own.

(16 marks plus 4 marks for SPaG and use of specialist terminology)

Sample extract

I agree that the use of gunpowder was the most important development in warfare in this period.

Gunpowder arrived in Europe in the 13th century and by 1700 cannon were a standard feature of every army. Early cannons were used to penetrate defensive walls that for centuries had been almost impossible to break through. Cannon were developed so they could fire longer distances and their reliability improved. By 1700, smaller cannons or light artillery were pulled around battlefields by horses.

From 1500, the first effective firearms using gunpowder were also in use. Matchlock muskets could pierce armour at 200 metres. Unlike archers, musketeers tired far less in battle as their work was less strenuous. Matchlock muskets were difficult to use in battles and took great courage as reloading took two minutes each time.

However, there were significant developments in weapons and the composition of armies used too. For example, the development of longbowmen. The longbow was an important development as its use was widespread in the Hundred Years' War. Longbowmen could fire 15 arrows a minute. At the Battle of Poitiers in 1356, the longbow was used to kill 2000 French mounted knights. During the Battle of Crécy, English longbowmen helped defeat a 30 000 strong French army with just 14 000 English troops.

Analysing the statement

The statement will always give a judgement on something. You decide whether you agree or not by weighing up points that support the statement with points that oppose it.

SPaG

In your answer to this question you will receive up to four marks for your spelling, punctuation and grammar and your use of specialist terms so check your work carefully. Remember to use as much specialist terminology as you can.

Links You can revise the development of gunpowder on pages 2 and 13.

Remember to give a clear indication whether you agree or disagree with the quotation. It doesn't matter whether you agree or not but you **must** state your opinion and then back it up.

This part of the answer concentrates on points that agree with the statement but it's important to look at points that disagree with the statement too. Here, the student goes on to write about developments in weapons, for example. Other important developments might include new strategy and formations.

Add your own knowledge where you can. This student uses the prompts in the question but also demonstrates some good knowledge of their own about warfare developments.

Practice

Put your skills and knowledge into practice with the following question.

> **Option 12: Warfare and British society, c1250–present**
> *and* London and the Second World War, 1939–45

SECTION A: London and the Second World War, 1939–45

Answer Questions 1 and 2.

1 Describe **two** features of air-raid shelters during the Blitz.

(4 marks)

You have to answer all questions in Section A. You should spend about 25 minutes on this section. Remember to leave five minutes or so to check your work when you've finished writing.

Feature 1

Guided   Air-raid shelters were sometimes public or

communal shelters

....

....

....

....

Links You can revise air-raid shelters on pages 21 and 27.

You need to identify **two** valid features and support each feature.

Feature 2

....

....

....

....

....

....

Your exam paper will have a separate space for each feature you need to describe.

Describe means you have to give an account of the main characteristic. You do not need to explain why the feature was important or what it was trying to achieve.

Practice

Put your skills and knowledge into practice with the following question.

2 (a) **Study Sources A and B on page 55.**

How useful are Sources A and B for an enquiry into government efforts to maintain public morale during the Blitz on London?

Explain your answer, using Sources A and B and your own knowledge of the historical context.　　**(8 marks)**

....

....

....

....

....

....

....

....

....

....

....

....

....

....

....

....

....

....

....

....

....

....

Spend some time studying and annotating the sources after you have read the question.

Links You can revise government efforts to maintain public morale on pages 27 and 28.

Make sure you use **both** sources in your answer and come to a judgement about how useful each source is.

You should give the strengths and weaknesses of each source for this particular enquiry, for example government efforts to maintain public morale during the Blitz.

Remember the key things to include for each source: content, provenance and your own knowledge.

See page 31 for more information on content and provenance.

For instance, you might describe Source A as being useful as an example of how local officials had more knowledge of the impact of the Blitz than central government.

Practice

Use this page to continue your answer to Question 2(a).

....

....

.... ◀ It's a good idea to conclude your answer by again stating how useful you think both sources are.

....

....

.... ◀ Remember, you don't need to compare the sources!

....

....

....

....

....

....

....

....

....

....

....

....

....

....

....

....

....

....

....

Practice

Put your skills and knowledge into practice with the following question.

2 (b) Study Source B on page 55.

How could you follow up Source B to find out more about the efforts made by the government to maintain public morale during the Blitz?

In your answer, you must give the question you would ask and the type of source you could use.

Complete the table below.   **(4 marks)**

Detail in Source B that I would follow up:

....

....

....

Question I would ask:

....

....

....

What type of source I could use:

....

....

....

How this might help answer my question:

....

....

....

....

Links You can revise government efforts to maintain public morale on pages 27 and 28.

You will be given a table with writing lines, which you should write your answer into. There are only four marks for this question so you don't need to spend time going into detail.

It's important that you focus on the enquiry given in the question here – there are several details in the source that you may like to follow up, but it has to be relevant to the government's efforts to maintain morale.

This question must relate to the detail you've given above.

There are many sources that you could suggest here, but you need to be able to say how your chosen source might help to answer your question. So make sure you pick a source you will be able to explain clearly.

See page 31 for types of source you could suggest.

Practice

Put your skills and knowledge into practice with the following question.

SECTION B: Warfare and British society, c1250–present

Answer Questions 3 and 4. Then answer EITHER Question 5 OR 6.

3 Explain **one** way in which the training in the army in 1250 was different from the training in the army in 1700. **(4 marks)**

 Links You can revise training in these periods on pages 3 and 14.

....

....

....

....

....

....

....

....

....

....

....

....

Remember to just give **one** way as the question asks. For example, you could focus on the professionalisation of soldiers by comparing the limited training of feudal troops with the development of a permanent standing army, the New Model Army.

You don't need to explain why they were different – just how! The question is only worth four marks and there's limited writing space so don't waste too much time on answering this question.

Practice

Put your skills and knowledge into practice with the following question.

4 Explain why there were changes in artillery in the period 1700–1918.

You may use the following in your answer:

- Industrialisation
- The Battle of the Somme, 1916

You **must** also use information of your own.   **(12 marks)**

Remember that Question 4 is all about **causation**: this means you are looking for relevant reasons.

Guided New discoveries in science and technology are important in explaining why artillery changed in this period. New technology also allowed more effective and mobile artillery on the battlefield.

For example, you might use the first prompt and write about how industrialisation led to new manufacturing methods.

 Links You can revise the development of artillery on pages 12 and 18.

There are 12 marks in total for this question. You don't have to use the prompts in the question in your answer but you **must** include your own information to answer the question fully.

You need to give more than one reason, and the best answers will show how different factors combined to prevent or bring about change.

Your explanations need to stay focused on answering the question. Although you might remember lots of detail, you need to focus on providing **reasons why**, not descriptions of.

Practice

Use this page to continue your answer to Question 4.

....
....
....
....
....
....
....
....
....
....
....
....
....
....
....
....
....
....
....
....
....
....
....
....
....
....
....
....
....

◀ Other detail you could include would be about the manufacturing methods of rifles, the impact of steel production and changes in the cost of the manufacture of weapons.

◀ Remember, the best answers to Question 4 will show a good knowledge of the key features and characteristics of the period, analyse the reasons for change or continuity **and** show how factors combined to bring about change or keep things the same.

◀ Make sure you support your explanation with a good range of accurate and relevant detail throughout your answer.

Practice

Use this page to continue your answer to Question 4.

Remember to include a short conclusion to your answer.

....
....
....
....
....
....
....
....
....
....
....
....
....
....
....
....
....
....
....
....
....
....
....
....
....
....
....
....
....
....
....

Practice

Put your skills and knowledge into practice with the following question.

Answer EITHER Question 5 OR Question 6.

Spelling, punctuation, grammar and use of specialist terminology will be assessed in this question.

EITHER

5 'The most important factor leading to changes in warfare in the perod c1800–c2000 was the development of new scientific ideas and technologies.'

How far do you agree? Explain your answer.

(16 marks, plus 4 marks for SPaG)

You may use the following in your answer:

- The atom bomb
- Satellite technology

You **must** also use information of your own.

OR

6 'The most important change in recruitment in the period c1800–c2000 was the introduction of conscription in 1916.'

How far do you agree? Explain your answer.

(16 marks, plus 4 marks for SPaG)

You may use the following in your answer:

- Cardwell's Army Reforms
- Military Service Act, 1916

You **must** also use information of your own.

If you decide to answer Question 5, turn to page 47. If you decide to answer Question 6, turn to page 51.

You have a choice of two questions for your final question of the exam. Each question is worth the same number of marks. Although one might immediately seem a question you can answer, do read both carefully to check your choice is the right one.

On the exam paper, Questions 5 and 6 will be on one page, and you will then turn to the next page to write your answer – like the layout here.

 Links You can revise the changes in warfare in this period on pages 13 and 19 and the changes in recruitment in this period on pages 14 and 20.

Total for Question 5/6 = 20 marks. There are 16 marks plus four marks for spelling, punctuation, grammar and use of specialist terminology.

Choosing a question

At the top of the first answer page there will be an instruction for you to indicate which of the two questions you have chosen to answer. You do this by making a cross in the box for Question 5 or Question 6.

Don't worry if you put a cross in the wrong box by mistake. Just put a line through the cross and then put a new cross in the right box.

Practice

Use this page to begin your answer to Question 5.

Indicate which question you are answering by marking a cross in the box. If you change your mind, put a line through the box and then indicate your new question with a cross.

Chosen question number: **Question 5** ☒   **Question 6** ☐

Guided   New developments in science and technology

were very important in changes in warfare in the period

c1800–c2000. Other factors including social attitudes,

and the role of government, were also important in

explaining changes in warfare, but new science and

technology was most important overall.

....

....

....

....

....

....

....

....

....

....

....

....

....

....

....

....

....

....

Remember to **only** answer **either** Question 5 **or** Question 6 in the exam.

As with Question 4, you do not have to use both or either of the two prompts provided by the question. If you do use them, remember that you **must** also include information of your own.

Plan your answer before you start writing. List factors that support the statement in the question and list other factors that go against the statement.

For example:

Support	Against
Mass standardised production.	Role of government expanded.
Invention of the atom bomb.	Advent of total war.
Use of satellite technology in warfare.	Introduction of conscription.

Practice

Use this page to continue your answer to Question 5.

....
....
....
....
....
....
....
....
....
....
....
....
....
....
....
....
....
....
....
....
....
....
....
....
....
....
....
....
....
....

Bring specific facts and details into your answer to show how well you understand the key features and characteristics that are involved in the question.

End your answer by saying **how far** you agree with the question statement and give support for your decision.

Remember, this question is where you will also receive marks for your spelling, punctuation and grammar and use of specialist terms so write and check your work carefully!

Practice

Use this page to continue your answer to Question 5.

Practice

Use this page to continue your answer to Question 5.

Practice

Use this page to start your answer to Question 6.

Indicate which question you are answering by marking a cross in the box. If you change your mind, put a line through the box and then indicate your new question with a cross.

Chosen question number: **Question 5** ☐   **Question 6** ☒

Guided Approaches to recruiting men to fight in conflict changed considerably in the period c1800–c2000. The government's methods for recruitment included a range of tactics, including making the army more professional. However, the scale of the fighting in the First World War, and the number of dead and injured soldiers, meant the government was forced to change the law and introduce conscription so that all men could be forced to join up.

....

....

....

....

....

....

....

....

....

....

....

....

....

....

....

....

....

....

Remember **only** to answer **either** Question 5 **or** Question 6 in the exam.

As with Question 4, you do not have to use both or either of the two prompts provided by the question. If you do use them, remember that you **must** also include information of your own.

Plan your answer before you start writing. List factors that support the statement in the question and list other factors that go against the statement.

For example:

Support	Against
Military Services Act, 1916 set out terms for conscription.	Recruitment methods of the early 19th century, including use of debtors and petty criminals as soldiers.
Numbers of dead/injured in First World War due to impact of new weapons.	Impact of Cardwell's reforms.
Social attitudes towards those who refused to fight.	Continuity of recruitment of officers in early 19th century.

Practice

Use this page to continue your answer to Question 6.

Bring specific facts and details into your answer to show how well you understand the key features and characteristics that are involved in the question.

End your answer by saying **how far** you agree with the question statement and give support for your decision.

Remember, this question is where you will also receive marks for your spelling, punctuation and grammar and use of specialist terms so write and check your work carefully!

Practice

Use this page to continue your answer to Question 6.

Practice

Use this page to continue your answer to Question 6.

....
....
....
....
....
....
....
....
....
....
....
....
....
....
....
....
....
....
....
....
....
....
....
....
....
....
....
....

Sources booklet

Use these sources to answer the questions in Section A (see pages 39–41).

Sources for use with Section A.

Source A: An extract from a local government report on the East End of London, September 1940.

The whole story of last weekend has been one of unplanned hysteria. The newspaper versions of life going on as normal in the East End are greatly distorted. There was no bread, no milk, no telephones. There was no humour or laughter. There was every excuse for people to be distressed. There was no understanding in the huge government buildings of central London for the tiny crumbled streets of massed populations.

Source B: A government propaganda poster from early in the Second World War, September 1939.

Answers

Where an exemplar answer is given, this is not necessarily the only correct response. In most cases there is a range of responses that can gain full marks.

SUBJECT CONTENT

Warfare and British society, c1250–present

c1250–c1500: Medieval warfare and English society

1. Composition of the army

Facts could include the following examples:

Infantry

- Infantry wore some protection in the form of a skull cap and leather jacket.
- They were engaged in hand-to-hand fighting using swords, pikes, battle axes, daggers, and so on.
- They were treated poorly compared to other soldiers.
- They were at the bottom of the social order.

Mounted knights

- Knights weakened the enemy in the first round of attack using tactics such as the mounted charge and rout and chase.
- They were the most powerful force on the battlefield.
- They fought on horseback and generally wore chainmail for protection.
- They used lances and swords for weapons.
- They were made up of noblemen and gentry.
- They provided service to their lord in return for the land they lived on.

Archers

- Archers were part of the infantry.
- They used crossbows and bows.
- They played a limited role at this time.
- They were used to attack enemy troops from a distance, weakening them alongside the cavalry, at the start of battle.

2. New weapons and formations

For example:

Gunpowder and cannon were important developments in the period c1250–c1500 even though they still had many limitations in their use. Gunpowder was used to fire cannon which, by the end of this period, was an important weapon for carrying out sieges. Cannon could be used to destroy defensive walls and their improved range and aim advanced their capability in attacks. Some types of cannon could fire balls high over defensive walls as new technology was developed.

3. Recruitment and training

For example:

Kings and army commanders could no longer rely on the feudal levy to supply enough cavalry. Previously, the feudal levy involved tenants giving 40 days' knight service and providing a knights' fee for land use. As these dues were more difficult to get, new types of recruitment methods came about. Increasingly, the king's subjects paid 'shield money' rather than providing military service. This meant that the king had the funds to pay for mercenaries as a form of recruitment.

4. Impact on civilians

For example, any two from:

- The king made forced purchases around the country and in theory had to pay civilians a fair price; however, this often wasn't honoured.
- Soldiers often stole food from civilians.
- Armies often set up near a town and demanded money from the townspeople and threatened them if they did not pay up. Captives had to pay ransoms to secure their release.
- Armies sometimes launched raids on towns and villages in enemy territory. This caused suffering and fear for civilians.
- Tax increases hurt civilians, but were probably not such a great problem compared to being recruited or having their belongings plundered by armies.
- The feudal summons to fight and the Assize of Arms were both ways of forced army recruitment. More civilians chose to pay money to the king to avoid fighting.

5. The Battle of Falkirk, 1298

For example, any three from:

- Wallace decided to face the enemy without enough troops; this was bad decision-making as he could have chosen to retreat and improve his chances for another time.
- This was the first battle where English archers showed their strength and Wallace was not prepared for this. Wallace's men had no armour, so the archers' attacks killed many of Wallace's troops.
- Wallace's strategy was flawed because he left his flanks vulnerable to English attack.
- Wallace failed to use his archers and cavalry effectively.
- Edward kept up the strength of his armies on the campaign by maintaining food supplies using ships at sea. This meant his army could fight more effectively at Falkirk.
- Edward had a larger fighting force – many of Wallace's army deserted, in particular the cavalry.

6. The Battle of Agincourt, 1415

For example:

- Use of archers: English longbowmen; their firing speed was huge, firing 100 000 arrows every minute, which inflicted great casualties on the French.
- Geography: English archers used the shelter of the woods to fire at the French and provoke a counterattack.
- French mistakes: The French cavalry tried to retreat but got caught up in their own infantry.
- French fatigue: The French infantry were exhausted because they had already struggled through thick mud and over the bodies of the fallen.
- English tactics: Henry used long sharpened stakes that were set in the ground and angled towards the oncoming French enemy to impale charging French horses.

c1500–c1700: Warfare and English society in the early modern period

7. Changes in the army

For example, your table might include:

Changes
- Archers were gradually replaced by musketeers due to new weapons technology.
- More training required for new weapons like muskets and cannons.
- Dragoons took on the role of the mounted archer.

Continuity
- Armies continued to be made up of around two-to-one infantry to cavalry.
- Armies continued to use mercenaries.
- Continued opposition to a standing army until the Civil War broke out.

8. Developments in weaponry

For example:
- In the mid-16th century, smaller firearms like the wheel-lock pistol were developed. The impact it had was that it made armour useless as it could not protect the soldier from the firepower of a pistol.
- The development of the cannon in the 1500s led to new engineering methods to build stronger defensive walls. England spent vast sums constructing new types of town defences. Earth-filled walls could withstand cannonballs without breaking. Walls were now angled to help cannonballs bounce off them.

9. The experience of war

For example:
- Oliver Cromwell proposed the idea of the New Model Army. They generally avoided forcing men to serve. Instead it was a professional army of volunteers. This meant civilians were not pressed into fighting in Cromwell's army.
- Through free quarter, armies would force civilian communities to feed and house troops, and just leave an IOU for what they had used. This led to real financial hardship for civilians.
- Armies sometimes marched on civilian crops which meant they were entirely ruined and this led to serious food shortages, as there was nothing to harvest. This damaged livelihoods. At least 55 000 civilians were made homeless during the Civil Wars.

10. The Battle of Naseby, 1645

For example, your mind map might include:

Strategy
- The Royalists underestimated the enemy.
- Charles I decided not to wait for reinforcements.
- Fairfax made good use of the terrain.

Leadership
- Fairfax was an inspirational general and fought with his men.
- Fairfax rallied the infantry and led the counterattack.
- NMA cavalry were well disciplined.
- Cromwell led his cavalry to make two decisive interventions.

Resources
- NMA recruited and trained the best cavalry in the war.
- Cromwell insisted on good soldiers for leaders.
- NMA outnumbered the Royalists.

c1700–c1900: Warfare and British society in the 18th and 19th centuries

11. Continuity and change in the army

1 For example:
- **Change:** The expansion of the armed forces.
  Explanation: Governments had an increasing role in organising the size and financing of the armed forces to defend British interests in the world.
- **Change:** Armies were transported to battle in steamships or steam trains.
  Explanation: New technology meant advanced transport methods were now available.

2 For example:
- **No change:** Generals struggled to adapt their tactics against overwhelming defensive firepower
  Explanation: A reliance on old tactics, despite the advancements in weaponry, led to high casualties.
- **No change:** Up to 1850, there was little improvement in the training of officers and troops.
  Explanation: Attitudes in society meant the officer class still resisted formal training and resented central interference in training and tactics.

12. Changes in weaponry

For example:

Heavy artillery saw some important changes in this period. New technology meant that new steel cannon were more durable than earlier bronze cannon. New technology impacted on how cannon were operated so, for example, breech-loading cannon reloaded five times faster than previous muzzle-loading cannon. This meant that they were far more effective in battles. From the 1890s, cannon with rifled barrels increased the range from hundreds of metres to up to 5 km, so the enemy could be targeted from much further away than before. New breakthroughs in chemistry meant that smokeless powder stopped smoke affecting aim or revealing the gun's position so it was easier to defend a position in battle.

13. Industrialisation

For example, your mind map might include:

Technology
- 1850s improved metal production.
- Increased cheap metals meant cheaper weapons.
- Factory production lines.
- Mass-produced identical parts at less cost.

Individuals
- John Wilkinson's gun manufacturing methods.
- Henry Bessemer's cheap steel.
- George Armstrong's breech-loading rifled cannon.

Communications
- Governments and army staff used telegraph; direct contact with generals on campaign.
- Newspaper reporters relied on telegraph information.

14. Reform in recruitment and training

For example, your table might include:

Recruitment
- Punishments, such as flogging, were abolished.
- The 1871 Regularisation of the Forces Act.
- Regiments were reorganised into regions, with local barracks for accommodation. This improved conditions and therefore helped recruitment.

Training
- 1860s saw an increase in officers joining the army via the Royal Military College at Sandhurst.
- Artillery and engineering officers trained at the Woolwich Military Academy.

15. Civilian experience of war

For example:
- Civilians were taxed more in wartime as the government raised taxes to cover war costs. There was less requisitioning but it was still sometimes necessary. The French Wars cost £25 million a year.
- Civilians were impacted by more wartime reporting of events. Reporting via telegraph and wartime photography brought the Crimean battlefields to life for the public in Britain. This had an important impact on public opinion as journalists showed first-hand the conditions soldiers and nurses were facing. Photographs made the war more obvious to the public who had previously only seen war artists' pictures.
- Barracking of increasing numbers of soldiers impacted on law and order in trade towns, as bands of soldiers disrupted trade and caused disturbances. Pay continued to be poor and the 1757 Militia Act was deeply unpopular.

16. The Battle of Waterloo, 1815

For example:

Wellington's strategy was successful. He chose a good defensive position. The battlefield was well suited to a defensive action as it was only about three miles across. Wellington's strategy to create two positions on the ridge to interrupt the French attack was a good tactical move. Wellington's defensive strategy also included the use of infantry squares with cannons positioned at the corners. The infantry were ordered to fire in rotation. At a crucial moment in the battle he switched from defence to attack and personally led his troops into the fiercest fighting. Eventually, with the help of the Prussians, Wellington was victorious.

17. The Battle of Balaclava, 1854

For example:

Older features
- Raglan's senior position as a result of commissions demonstrates a reliance on old recruitment methods.
- Raglan relied on old strategies for the battle (such as cavalry charges) and did not take the necessary steps to prepare for new challenges.

Newer features
- The British infantry used Minié rifles. The power of new weapons, like the Minié rifles, in defence became a central characteristic of warfare after the Crimean campaign.
- A military railway and steamships transported British supplies during the campaign.

c1900–present: Warfare and British society in the modern era

18. The modern army

For example:
- Changing army size: The army expanded during the First and Second World Wars, but is much smaller now.
- Infantry: made up two-thirds of the army in 1914. They are still the troops most likely to fight on the ground but the relative number in the army is fewer, reduced to a quarter of Britain's army in the present day.
- Role of the cavalry is now carried out by tank units.
- Modern-day reliance on aircraft and tanks, which now fulfil a similar function to the artillery previously.
- Since the Second World War, the role of logistics has increased. In the modern day, the Royal Logistics Corps accounts for about 15 per cent of army personnel.

19. Impact of modern developments

For example:
- Changes in high-tech weapons have had a devastating impact on warfare. The casualty rates have increased massively, leading to 'Mutually Assured Destruction' should they be used. New scientific understanding has been used with devastating effect, such as in the development of the first atom bomb.
- New technologies have also changed the nature of warfare as there is more emphasis on surveillance methods. Surveillance technology means that missiles can be guided to targets and bombs are sent by 'stealth' aircraft, fighter jets and drones. These 'smart' bombs are much more accurate and commanders can, in theory, target specific individuals and groups rather than bomb entire communities.

20. Modern recruitment and training

For example:

Recruitment
- Early in 1916, the Military Service Act introduced conscription in the First World War.
- Women were recruited into the forces for the first time. In 1916, they worked in Voluntary Aid Detachments behind the front line as nurses and, from 1917–19, women were recruited into the armed forces in women's corps.
- In the Second World War, 212 000 women served in a range of military-based roles.

Training
- In 1948, 'National Service' was introduced. This meant all men aged 17–21 had to complete 18 months of military training and service in the armed forces.
- In the modern day, basic initial training lasts 14 weeks. Training for specialist units lasts up to a year more.
- In the modern day, about 80 per cent of officers join the army as graduates.

21. Modern warfare and civilians

Civilians in the Second World War faced, as they did in the First World War, rationing and conscription, though in the Second World War men could choose to work in the mining industry instead of fighting. While there were some limited attacks on Britain during the First World War, the attacks on the Home Front in the Second World War were on a much greater scale. The Home Guard, the Civil Defence and the Women's Voluntary Service coordinated the defence against invasion. Precautions also had to be taken against the frequent air attacks, like those of the Blitz. For example, gas masks and air-raid shelters were provided, and blackouts and curfews were enforced. Many civilians, including children, were evacuated out of the cities, and two million homes were destroyed between 1940 and 1941 alone.

22. Attitudes in society

For example:

- In the First World War, propaganda often concentrated on German atrocities. In contrast, during the Second World War, the government strategy was to focus on the horrors of war and victory. Posters were often used to encourage support for the war effort and to build morale.
- Attitudes to COs changed to some extent. Tribunals were willing to allow absolute exemption from war-related work in the Second World War, unlike in the First World War, where men were more often imprisoned or threatened with the death penalty for refusing to undertake war work. But there was still a lot of hostility to COs; they were often seen as letting down their country.

23. The Western Front and the Somme, 1916

For example:
- A lot of the British infantry were new volunteers and lacked experience in trench warfare.
- The German trench system was too strong for the British artillery, which failed to have any significant impact on German defences before troops went over the top.
- The barbed wire protecting the trenches in No Man's Land remained intact, so men were caught in it as they tried to advance.
- The German trench system was extensive; it included 12 lines of parallel trenches and dugouts, and a network of useful tunnels that helped keep their front line supplied. This made them very hard to capture and hold successfully.

24. The Iraq War, 2003

For example, your table might include:

Weapons
- Smart bombs and cruise missiles can be controlled and adjusted to steer them to the target while they are in flight.
- These types of bomb have changed warfare as they can be sent to a more specific target than was the case using conventional technology.
- The British used tanks that were fitted with computer-controlled laser-assisted guns. This use of lasers has changed warfare as it has led to greater accuracy in targeted attacks.

Surveillance techniques
- Ground pilots use cameras to operate drones which are used for reconnaissance and bombing. More detailed reconnaissance has changed warfare as it gives commanders more information which allows them to make better-informed decisions.
- The Coalition used satellites to intercept Iraqi communications. They also provided Coalition troops with pictures from the ground. The use of satellites means that strategy can be based on greater knowledge of what is actually happening.

London and the Second World War, 1939–45
The historic environment
25. London: a target city

For example:
- London is the base of government which the enemy wanted to undermine.
- The government in London handled lots of important aspects of the war in practical and logistical terms.
- London was the centre of industrial production and a transport hub.
- Attacks on London undermined morale as attacking well-known places of historical interest made people feel that the Germans were attacking the things that were considered important to the British people.
- London is densely populated and high civilian casualties would undermine morale.

26. The nature of the Blitz

For example:

The First Blitz against London was focused on industry and transport. The heaviest bombing in 1940–41 was on the East End areas of London. The Germans then shifted their tactics, making all of London a target. They used incendiaries which led to widespread fires. They also used high-explosive bombs and mines that were carried to the target using a parachute. The Germans wanted to destroy civilian morale and used a range of weapons to spread fear and panic. Later in the war, 1944–45, they changed the type of weapons they used. They launched flying bombs, called V1s, and rockets, called V2s, from positions in northern France. These attacks were very difficult to stop and struck with little warning, which badly harmed civilian morale.

27. Impact on civilian life

For example:
- Morale was kept high by not reporting some news like the disaster at South Hallsville School.
- Wartime audiences in cinemas increased by more than half. People were keen to watch information films presented in cinemas and to carry on with aspects of their lives that were more normal. The government used cinema as a propaganda opportunity to promote unity among people.
- The government understood that leisure time was important for morale. Large dance halls stayed open throughout the war. People took the opportunity to try to socialise and have some fun when they could.

28. London's response

For example:

Measure: Government

Helped by: The government stayed in London to show Londoners that they would not be abandoned.

Measure: Protecting national treasures

Helped by: National treasures and important artworks were kept hidden somewhere safe, for example, the British Museum stored artifacts in a disused Underground station. This made sure that people felt their national history was being protected.

Measure: Rations

Helped by: The 'Dig for Victory' campaign ensured that everyone was encouraged to grow their own food to boost what was available in rations. Public spaces were turned into plots for growing vegetables, which helped people feel that everyone was doing their bit for the war.

PRACTICE

38. Practice

For example:

Air-raid shelters were sometimes public or communal shelters built from brick or concrete by councils. These shelters were constructed in the middle of streets but many people felt unsafe as they were quite exposed to bombing raids.

Some air-raid shelters were positioned in people's gardens; these were called domestic shelters, like Anderson shelters. These were provided by the council for each house and were constructed from steel and earth.

39. Practice

For example:

Source A is very useful for finding out how the government maintained public morale. It provides evidence that local government authorities wanted to find out about the situation caused by the Blitz bombings and reported on it. Clearly the authorities were concerned about how their local communities were coping and needed information in order to decide how best to deal with the hardships and to maintain public morale. Source A is useful because, as a report that was for internal local government use, rather than for wider publication, it reveals some harsh truths about the problems. The report highlights problems including shortages of basics like bread and milk. It also states that the central government authorities had 'no understanding' of how 'massed populations' were suffering. This is useful as it suggests that there was a tension in government between the local and national government systems in their efforts to maintain morale. The source is useful as it directly challenges the reports in the media that presented the situation in a far more positive light. I also know that newspaper reports and photographs about the Blitz were censored. Government agencies did not allow photographs of bombed-out homes or pictures of casualties to be published as they feared the negative impact on morale.

Source B is quite useful for understanding the measures taken by the government to improve morale. Posters were widely used in the war to give clear and simple messages that everyone could understand. In this poster, the message is very direct. It is the responsibility of everyone; this is emphasised by the fact that 'Your' is emphasised each time. It is useful as it shows how the government needed ordinary people to accept their role in the war effort as a duty and this included a duty to remain cheerful despite the hardships and suffering that they experienced. However, the limits of the poster are that it does not show how people reacted to these instructions from the government or what the impact of these types of posters really was on people's state of mind.

41. Practice

For example:

Detail in Source B that I would follow up: I would follow up the detail 'Your cheerfulness, Your resolution'.

Question I would ask: Were people during the Blitz cheerful and resolute about winning the war?

What type of source I could use: I would use autobiographies of people who lived through the Blitz to find out how they dealt with the impact of the bombing.

How this might help answer my question: This source might help me answer the question because it will show whether their morale was actually high or low and if their resolve to carry on and appear cheerful was actually crumbling away.

42. Practice

For example:

In the 13th century there was little formal training. Infantry were told they should be skilled with weapons, but there was almost no organised training. Although the cavalry were already trained in skills, like horsemanship and the use of lances, there was no formal training in how to fight in large, disciplined groups.

By 1700, training was very different. England effectively had a standing army, the New Model Army. Troops were well trained and disciplined in their battle techniques. Training was given by soldiers who had proved their merit in fighting rather than by those of high social status.

43. Practice

For example:

New discoveries in science and technology are important in explaining why artillery changed in this period. New technology also allowed more effective and mobile artillery on the battlefield. Industrialisation is another important cause of the changes in artillery between 1700 and the First World War.

By 1700, lighter bronze-barrelled field guns were developed, which had lighter gun carriages. This meant that the artillery was more mobile around the battlefield and could be used against enemy infantry. This is an example of how new technology allowed materials to be used in artillery in new ways to make it more effective. As a result, commanders experimented with new battle techniques to make use of the more mobile field guns.

In the 19th century, new thinking and improvements in the manufacture and functioning of rifles were applied to artillery to improve their accuracy. For example, the use of rifled barrels, which were a series of spiralled grooves down the barrel of the gun that spun the projectile and thereby increased accuracy. By the mid-19th century, technological advances in the manufacture of steel had a direct impact by reducing the cost of artillery manufacture. For example, Bessemer invented a process where steel could be produced for approximately a tenth of the previous cost.

By the time of the First World War, industrialisation had revolutionised the quantity and transportation of artillery to the front line. There was continuity from the previous century in the type of artillery being used, but the scale of the production of that weaponry was transformed. For example, at the Battle of the Somme, Haig ordered a week-long bombardment of German positions prior to a British infantry attack. During this time, 1.7 million shells were fired.

In conclusion, the main causes of changes in artillery in the period were new developments in technology that relied on new scientific thinking and engineering. Also, industrialisation had an important impact on the availability of new technology and the possibilities it presented for changes in artillery in warfare.

47. Practice

For example:

New developments in science and technology were very important in changes in warfare in the period c1800–c2000. Other factors including social attitudes, and the role of government, were also important in explaining changes in warfare, but new science and technology was most important overall.

The period 1800–50 saw continuity in the impact of science and technology as there were few changes in weapons and tactics. However, in the second half of the 19th century, the process of industrialisation created advances in the effectiveness and firepower of weapons and mass standardised production methods for armaments and ammunitions. The cost of raw materials, particularly steel, was dramatically lowered so production was cheaper and weapons could be used in much greater numbers.

By the 20th century, the most important technological development was the invention of the atom bomb. Atomic technology relied on breakthroughs in understanding of nuclear physics. The development of the nuclear age of warfare had a great impact on warfare. The use of nuclear weapons in Japan in 1945 brought the Second World War to a sudden end and led to a greater concern by the public about the impact of war on civilians and the long-term human and environmental effects of nuclear war. The ongoing fear of nuclear war after 1945 had an important impact on warfare as ordinary people put pressure on governments to stop nuclear tests and to scale back their nuclear weapons arsenals. The development of weapons of mass destruction meant that warfare had changed greatly and could now lead to the complete destruction of the planet itself.

With the 21st century, scientific discoveries and new technologies have changed warfare further as new laser-guided bombs using satellite technology mean that greater bombing precision is possible. Bombs can be used for a specific target rather than mass bombing an area to destroy a target. Also, global positioning satellites allow cruise missiles to be fired from up to 2400 km away but with an accuracy of just 10 metres. This has changed warfare as enemies can be attacked from long distance with less risk to the operators who stay out of range from enemy armaments. Furthermore, with satellites now used for observation, generals are no longer required to be positioned in the battlefield and can give orders about war strategy from a safe distance with a much clearer picture of the battle.

Although science and technology have been important in changing warfare in the period c1800–c2000, I believe that others factors have played a role too. The role of the government in changing warfare was significant in this period. For example, total warfare in the First World War meant that, for the first time, the entire economy was focused on war production. The scale of the losses and the economic costs of the war were greater than anything Britain had previously experienced. Military deaths of British soldiers are estimated at around 800 000. The mobilisation of the Home Front ensured that civilians were expected to do their bit for the war effort as rationing was introduced and production was concentrated on war needs. Conscription was also introduced by the Military Service Act (1916). A similar thing happened in the Second World War as well. Once again, total warfare led to a war economy, rationing, the mobilisation of the Home Front and conscription.

However, while the government played a role in changes in warfare, science and technology had the biggest impact on warfare in this period.

51. Practice

For example:

Approaches to recruiting men to fight in conflict changed considerably in the period c1800–c2000. The government's methods for recruitment included a range of tactics, including making the army more professional. However, the scale of the fighting in the First World War, and the number of dead and injured soldiers, meant the government was forced to change the law and introduce conscription so that all men could be forced to join up.

In 1800, Britain had a standing army that was paid wages on a regular basis. During the early 19th century, the methods of recruitment saw a lot of continuity. The quality of officers was often poor because officers bought their commissions. High-rank positions were only given to nobility. Other ranks could sign up for 'short' enlistments of 8–12 years or for life. The army still found it difficult to recruit enough men. In wartime, criminals and debtors were signed up if they agreed to serve in the army instead of staying behind bars. The quality of recruits was low and officers relied on hard discipline to keep control. Recruiting offices often ignored age and physical fitness tests. In the Boer War, 1899, many recruits were malnourished and physically weak as a result.

In the later 19th century, the role of government increased and impacted on recruitment. New laws were introduced to try to help the problem of army recruitment, known as Cardwell's Army Reforms. The 1870 Army Act meant lower ranks joined up for 12 years, six in the army and six as a reserve soldier. After 12 years of service, soldiers could resign without an army pension. These changes meant that Britain now had a good, regular supply of trained soldiers, so the problem of recruitment was improved. The Regularisation of the Forces Act 1871 meant regiments were reorganised into regions, and stayed in local barracks. Every army regiment had to have two linked battalions – one serving at home and one abroad. This lowered the time on duty abroad. These changes improved conditions for recruits and helped recruitment levels as the prospect of joining the army no longer meant such long periods away from Britain.

However, conscription was the biggest change in recruitment. By 1916, during the First World War, the number of volunteer soldiers was not sufficient to meet the needs of the war. The casualty rate was so high that thousands of men were needed every week. Early in 1916, the Military Service Act brought in conscription – which meant enlistment became law. All unmarried men, aged 18–41, had to serve. In May 1916, the Act was changed to include married men as well. The sick, or those in vital jobs, were sometimes let off. Some men refused to join up and were punished harshly as a result. Conscription ended in 1918 with the end of the war.

In 1939, conscription was again a major change in how soldiers were recruited. At the start of the Second World War, the volunteer army was not big enough, so conscription was reintroduced. The National Service Act meant all men, aged 18–41, were required to join up. Over a million men were conscripted into the British army in the first year of the conflict alone. Conscription continued until 1948, and was then replaced by 'National Service'. This meant all men aged 17–21 had to complete 18 months of military training and service in the armed forces. Conscription ended in 1960, and the army went back to a voluntary permanent standing force.

To conclude, by the 19th century, recruitment methods were changing as the role of government grew and new laws were introduced that made recruitment easier. However, the First World War, and the huge casualties involved, meant the government introduced conscription. This was the most important turning point in recruitment as, for the first time, all able-bodied young men were required by law to join up on a scale never seen before. Therefore, I agree that the introduction of conscription in 1916 was the most important change in recruitment in this period.

Published by Pearson Education Limited, 80 Strand, London, WC2R 0RL.

www.pearsonschoolsandfecolleges.co.uk

Copies of official specifications for all Pearson qualifications may be found on the website: qualifications.pearson.com

Text and illustrations © Pearson Education Ltd 2017
Typeset and illustrated by Techset Ltd, Gateshead
Produced by Out of House Publishing
Cover illustration by Eoin Coveney

The right of Victoria Payne to be identified as author of this work has been asserted by her in accordance with the Copyright, Designs and Patents Act 1988.

Content written by Rob Bircher, Brian Dowse and Kirsty Taylor is included.

First published 2017

20 19 18 17

10 9 8 7 6 5 4 3 2 1

British Library Cataloguing in Publication Data

A catalogue record for this book is available from the British Library

ISBN 978 1 292 17645 1

Printed in Slovakia by Neografia

Acknowledgements

The authors and publisher would like to thank the following individuals and organisations for their kind permission to reproduce copyright material.

Photographs

(Key: b-bottom; c-centre; l-left; r-right; t-top)

Alamy Stock Photo: World History Archive 04, Interfoto 15, Alex Segre 28r, Maurice Savage 32; **Getty Images:** Topical Press Agency/Stringer/Archive Photos 55; **Mary Evans Picture Library:** Roger Mayne Archive 21, Illustrated London News Ltd 281

All other images © Pearson Education

Notes from the publisher

1. While the publishers have made every attempt to ensure that advice on the qualification and its assessment is accurate, the official specification and associated assessment guidance materials are the only authoritative source of information and should always be referred to for definitive guidance.

   Pearson examiners have not contributed to any sections in this resource relevant to examination papers for which they have responsibility.

2. Pearson has robust editorial processes, including answer and fact checks, to ensure the accuracy of the content in this publication, and every effort is made to ensure this publication is free of errors. We are, however, only human, and occasionally errors do occur. Pearson is not liable for any misunderstandings that arise as a result of errors in this publication, but it is our priority to ensure that the content is accurate. If you spot an error, please do contact us at resourcescorrections@pearson.com so we can make sure it is corrected.